Retrain Your Brain:
Cognitive Behavioral Therapy
—— IN 7 WEEKS ——

Retrain Your Brain

Cognitive Behavioral Therapy in 7 WEEKS

A Workbook for Managing Depression and Anxiety

SETH J. GILLIHAN, PHD

ALTHEA PRESS

Quick-Start Guide

Is this book for you? Check the boxes that often describe you:

☐   I have trouble sleeping.

☐   I feel like I have nothing to look forward to.

☐   I have a hard time unwinding.

☐   I'm not as interested in things I used to enjoy.

☐   I dread the next attack of anxiety.

☐   I struggle to concentrate and make decisions.

☐   I feel guilty and down on myself.

☐   I'm terrified of certain objects, animals, or situations.

☐   It's hard for me to find energy and motivation.

☐   I worry more than I need to.

☐   I often feel tense and anxious.

☐   I avoid things I need to do because they make me anxious.

☐   It's hard for me to control my worry.

☐   I feel extremely nervous is some social situations, and avoid them if I can.

If you checked several of the boxes, read on to learn about CBT and take part of the therapeutic process into your own hands.

For my father's father,
CPO Frank Rollin Gillihan
(1919–1967)

Contents

Foreword

RESEARCH HAS SHOWN THAT COGNITIVE-BEHAVIORAL THERAPY (CBT) is the most effective treatment for depressive and anxiety disorders, surpassing medication and other types of therapy in its ability to ameliorate suffering and prevent relapse. But what is CBT, and how does it work?

It's difficult to appreciate CBT's power to heal until you have seen it in action. In my clinical work, I have witnessed people debilitated by these disorders awaken as they learn cognitive-behavioral techniques.

For example, one of my clients, a 65-year-old woman who had suffered from severe depression for 30 years, arrived at my door feeling hopeless, frustrated, and entirely skeptical that I could help her "think her way out of it." In her mind, she was a victim of a cruel genetic lottery, and there was nothing she (or I) could do to improve her mood.

Yet within a few sessions she became aware of her thought processes and came to acknowledge that many of her assumptions about herself were not based in fact. She began to question these assumptions before jumping to conclusions and to consider other possibilities. She discovered that her thoughts were not always entirely accurate, and she learned how to look for evidence before believing her initial judgments.

This awareness of her thinking patterns led to small but profound changes in the way she related to her husband. As her marriage began to improve, she felt secure enough to reevaluate her interpretations of others' reactions to her, and she began to understand that the lens through which she experienced the world was distorted. Through CBT, she was able to restructure her thought processes so that she could accept the world, and herself, on more accurate grounds.

Gradually, she gained the confidence to start socializing again and to reach out to family members she thought had given up on her. She was pleasantly surprised by the reaction she received from them. I watched her transform from someone who could barely muster the energy to go for a walk to someone engaged in social and family events, and someone who looked forward to the next day. Such is the potential of CBT to transform lives.

People often seek help for depression and anxiety in books but abandon these books when they encounter academic jargon or overly long explanations of psychological theory, or feel disheartened by the sheer length of the books. For those struggling with the weight of low mood or fraught with the exhaustion of anxiety, a thick book written in abstract language can feel overwhelming. But in these pages, Dr. Gillihan has provided us with a simple, succinct, and stress-free workbook. It is ideal for people who feel exhausted or defeated by their struggles. In nine easy-to-read chapters, Dr. Gillihan instills confidence and mastery in his readers by breaking down cognitive-behavioral strategies into easily digestible concepts and exercises.

I have known Dr. Gillihan for 15 years and have witnessed firsthand his compassion and empathy for patients who reach out to him for help at their most vulnerable moments. At their lowest point, he can provide the care they need and gently equip them with the skills to help themselves. Now, more than a decade after we were in school together, I appreciate being able to discuss clinical issues with Dr. Gillihan as he draws on his broad experience helping patients and their families fight anxiety and depression. He has written extensively on the topic of depression and anxiety, publishing over 40 academic and clinical manuscripts, and he is coauthor of the book *Overcoming OCD: A Journey to Recovery*.

Engaging in the process of CBT is indeed a journey, one that can be challenging and arduous, but one that is also exciting and rewarding. Like all difficult journeys it is best traveled with an experienced and knowledgeable guide. I can think of no better person to lead you on this journey than Dr. Seth Gillihan.

LUCY F. FAULCONBRIDGE, PHD

Introduction

HOW CAN I HELP PEOPLE SUFFER LESS and live more fully? This question drove me to become a psychotherapist. I still remember when I discovered the answer as a master's student. I was in the library late one night, reading up on something called cognitive-behavioral therapy (CBT). During that study session, I learned how CBT can help us replace thoughts and behaviors that aren't working for us with new ones that work better.

The treatment approach seemed so reasonable, so collaborative between therapist and client, so respectful of those seeking help. With its implicit assumption that we can use what's whole in us to heal what's broken, CBT appealed to my humanistic leanings. CBT programs were also well tested, so I could be confident they would help many people. I knew right away that I'd found my home as a therapist.

After my master's, I wanted more specialized training in CBT, so I pursued my PhD at the University of Pennsylvania—a school where many of the best-tested cognitive-behavioral treatments were developed. Over the next 12 years, I studied, practiced, and researched CBT for anxiety and depression, first as a doctoral student, and then as a faculty member at Penn. Over and over I was struck by the power of CBT to help people break through major barriers in their lives.

What I hadn't anticipated was how personally useful the principles of CBT would be. Life is hard for all of us, and I've had my share of panic attacks, depressed moods, insomnia, anxiety, stress, and crushing disappointment. I've found that the tools of CBT work as well for the therapist as for the client.

I've been on the other side of therapy, too. I know the value of having another person to listen to us, to validate our perspective, to gently challenge us when needed, to give us a place where we can say anything and be accepted as we are. If you've found a good therapist, you know exactly what I'm talking about.

Many people who come to my office also have had therapy before. They may have explored their childhoods, identified patterns in their closest relationships, and gained valuable insights. They probably found the therapy very helpful, even lifesaving. And yet they've sought out a CBT therapist because, for some reason, *they haven't been able to make the changes they want.*

Maybe they haven't been able to break their habit of avoiding uncomfortable situations. Or they continue to be plagued by constant worry. Or they can't stop their habitual self-criticism. What they're often looking for are tools and skills to address the issues that they're well aware of. CBT can help a person transform insight into change.

I want as many people as possible to experience the power of CBT to make their struggles more manageable. Unfortunately, many people simply don't know that short-term, highly effective psychological treatment is available. Others have trouble finding a therapist who provides CBT. Still others can't afford treatment. This book is part of an effort to make CBT more readily available to those who need it.

My goal in writing this book is to introduce you to a set of skills that can help relieve anxiety and depression. If you've read other CBT books, you might find this one to be different in some ways. I've strived to make the material easy to relate to, without unnecessary information.

I've also organized the topics around a seven-week plan that builds on itself week by week. Why seven weeks? The structure of this book is similar to what I do with my clients: In the initial session(s), we develop a solid treatment plan, and then work on learning the basic skills of CBT in the next few sessions. The rest of treatment focuses on applying these skills. This book is designed in the same way: Gain the CBT skills you need as quickly as possible, and then continue using the skills on your own—in other words, *learn to be your own therapist.*

CBT has helped countless individuals live better lives. Can everyone benefit from CBT? Probably not. But I've found that the people who do well with it tend to do three things: First, they show up—it's probably a given that coming to treatment consistently is a good thing. Second, they bring a healthy skepticism; being a "true believer" in the treatment isn't necessary to benefit from it. And finally, they are willing to try out some new things.

I invite you to do the same. "Showing up" in this case means bringing your full attention and intention to this work, because you owe yourself nothing less. I encourage you to dive into the plan and see if it works for you. If you do these things, my guess is that you'll join the majority of people who get tremendous benefit from CBT.

Let's get started.

PART ONE

BEFORE YOU BEGIN

Before we dive into our seven-week program, it helps to know a little bit about CBT—what it is, where it came from, and how it's used. It also helps to have a sense of what kinds of conditions are most effectively treated with CBT.

CHAPTER ONE

Getting Familiar with Cognitive Behavioral Therapy (CBT)

In this chapter, I'll describe CBT, including a brief summary of how it was developed, and discuss how therapists might apply it. I'll also review its effectiveness. By the end of this chapter, you should know the "big idea" behind CBT and what makes it powerful.

First, let's consider Ted's experience:

Ted is walking through the woods on a cool spring morning. The cherry and magnolia trees are in full bloom, and he feels the warmth of the sun's rays as they filter through the trees. The sound of birds singing fills the air.

As Ted walks, he comes upon a wooden foot bridge. It's wide and solid looking, about the length of a school bus. The bridge passes over a large creek 30 or 40 feet below.

As Ted nears the bridge, he feels a sudden tightening in his chest and stomach. He peers down at the creek and immediately gets light-headed. It feels like he's not getting enough air. "I can't do it," he thinks. "I can't cross this bridge." He looks across the bridge to where the trail continues on to the vistas he was looking forward to.

As he tries to collect himself, Ted wonders why this is happening. He didn't used to have problems with bridges, until he was stuck in traffic on an enormous suspension bridge during a powerful thunderstorm. Now these attacks happen often.

After he feels a bit calmer, he tries to muster courage enough to cross the bridge. A few paces into it, he's overwhelmed by fear and runs back, disappointed, and he heads back to his car.

If Ted had pursued treatment in the first half of the twentieth century, chances are he would have been in psychoanalysis, a therapy pioneered by Sigmund Freud and further developed by his followers. Psychoanalysis is based on a Freudian understanding of the mind, which includes tenets such as:

- Early life experiences are powerful determinants of personality.
- Important parts of the mind are "buried" far below our conscious awareness.
- Our animal drives of lust and aggression are at war with our consciences, leading to anxiety and internal conflict.

Accordingly, Freud intended psychoanalysis as a way to understand and address "unconscious" internal conflicts rooted in childhood.

In psychoanalysis sessions, Ted would probably lie down on a couch and talk for most of the hour, with occasional comments or questions from his psychoanalyst. He might explore what the bridge represents, with guidance from the analyst. For example, what from his childhood does he associate with the bridge? Did his mom and dad encourage him to explore, or did he receive mixed messages about "being brave" but also "staying close to Mom"?

At some point, according to Freud, the treatment would address Ted's feelings toward the analyst, which would be interpreted as being "transferred" from earlier relationships (particularly with his mom or dad). Ted might see his psychoanalyst four days a week, for years.

In addition to being a long-term treatment, there was scant evidence about how well psychoanalysis worked. Thus Ted might spend years in a treatment with unknown effectiveness. Later developments in the field of psychotherapy were intended to address these shortcomings.

A Brief History of CBT

The second half of the twentieth century brought with it a very different approach to addressing the type of fear Ted experienced. Writers and researchers envisioned a form of therapy built around recent scientific discoveries, first in the field of animal behavior and a little later in the area of cognition, or thought. Let's take a look at each of these forms of therapy and consider how they merged.

BEHAVIOR THERAPY

A powerful science of animal learning and behavior was developed starting in the early twentieth century. First, Ivan Pavlov discovered how animals learn that two things go together. In his 1906 study, the experimenter would ring a bell and then give a dog food; after a few rounds of pairing bell and food, the dog would start to drool just from hearing the bell. It had learned that the bell signaled food was coming.

A few decades later, scientists like B. F. Skinner were discovering how behavior is shaped. What makes us more likely to do some things and less likely to do others? The results are now well known: Punish an action to stop it; reward an action to encourage it. Taken together, the findings of Pavlov, Skinner, and their colleagues provided several tools for influencing animal behavior—including human behavior.

Behavioral scientists in the mid-twentieth century saw a tremendous opportunity to use these principles in the service of mental health. Instead of years on the couch, maybe a few sessions of focused behavioral treatment could help individuals overcome anxiety and other issues.

Perhaps the best-known early pioneer of behavioral therapy is South African psychiatrist Joseph Wolpe, pioneer of a behavior-based anxiety treatment called systematic desensitization. Also hailing from South Africa was Arnold Lazarus, a collaborator with Wolpe who designed a "multimodal" therapy that integrated behavior therapy into a more comprehensive approach.

How would these and other behavioral therapists explain and treat Ted's struggle? They would likely say something like this:

Well, Ted, it looks like you've learned to be afraid of bridges, maybe because you had that frightening experience on a bridge and now associate bridges with danger. Every time you approach a bridge, you start to panic, which feels really uncomfortable, to say the least. So understandably you try to escape the situation.

Every time you escape, you get a sense of relief—you avoided something that feels awful—so you're rewarded for avoiding. While avoidance feels better in the short term, it doesn't help you get across the bridge, because that reward strengthens the habit of avoiding.

Here's what we're going to do, if you're up for it. We'll make a list of situations that trigger your fear, and we'll rate each activity for how challenging it would be. Then we'll work through the list systematically, starting with the easier ones and working up to the harder ones. When you face your fears, they diminish. It shouldn't take long before you're feeling more comfortable on bridges, as your brain learns that bridges actually aren't that dangerous.

Notice that Ted's behavior therapist doesn't mention Ted's childhood or unconscious conflicts—he focuses on the behavior that keeps Ted stuck, and on changing that behavior to get him better.

COGNITIVE THERAPY

A second wave of short-term treatment, developed in the 1960s and '70s, emphasized the power of thoughts to drive our emotions and actions.

The two men generally considered to be the fathers of cognitive therapy could hardly be more different. Albert Ellis was a confrontational and irreverent psychologist; psychiatrist Aaron Beck, on the other hand, is a lifelong academic with a fondness for bow ties. Yet somehow they developed, independent of each other, strikingly similar therapies.

The premise of cognitive therapy is that maladies like anxiety and depression are driven by our thoughts. To understand how we feel, we have to know what we're thinking. If we suffer from overwhelming anxiety, our thoughts are probably filled with danger.

For example, when Ted saw a bridge and felt extreme fear, his experience was:

Bridge → Fear

From a cognitive therapy perspective, a crucial step is missing: Ted's *interpretation* of what a bridge represents:

Bridge → "I'm going to lose control and jump off the side" → Fear

In light of Ted's beliefs, his fear makes perfect sense. That doesn't mean his thoughts are accurate, but if we understand what he's thinking, it's easy to see why he feels afraid.

When we're depressed, our thoughts are often hopeless and self-defeating. Again, in cognitive therapy, it's important to figure out how our thoughts contribute to our low mood. For example, Jan might have had this experience:

Got honked at while driving → Felt bad for rest of day

What actually drove her low mood wasn't getting honked at, but the story she told herself about what it meant:

Got honked at while driving →
"I can't do anything right" → Felt bad for rest of day

Again, the emotional responses make sense when we know what the thoughts are.

Our thoughts and feelings go hand in hand. The crucial insight of cognitive therapy is that *by changing how we think, we can change our feelings and behaviors.*

Let's examine what a cognitive therapist might say to Ted:

It sounds like your mind is overestimating how dangerous bridges are. You believe that either the bridge is going to fail or you're going to get so scared, you'll do something impulsive like hurl yourself over the side.

What I'd like to do with you is look at the evidence. We can find out if bridges are as dangerous as it feels like they are. We'll just gather some data—from research, from your experience, and from experiments we can do together. For example, we could go on a bridge that you find difficult but manageable, and see if what you're afraid of actually happens.

Chances are you'll learn fairly quickly that bridges are sound, and there's no realistic chance of your acting on an impulse and doing something awful. As your mind adjusts its estimate of the actual danger, you'll feel more comfortable on bridges and can get back to how your life used to be.

COGNITIVE BEHAVIORAL THERAPY: AN INEVITABLE INTEGRATION

As you read the descriptions of behavioral and cognitive therapy for Ted, you might have thought that they don't sound all that different. And you would be right—our thoughts and actions are connected, and it's hard to imagine changing one without affecting the other.

Behavior therapy and cognitive therapy share the same aims and often use similar tools. It's telling that the names of the therapies have changed to include both cognitive and behavioral aspects, as Beck and Ellis each added the word "behavior" to their signature treatments. Even the professional organizations have gotten onboard, as the former American Association for Behavioral Therapy is now the Association for Behavioral and Cognitive Therapies.

Attention! If you are suffering from serious depression, having thoughts of hurting yourself, or experiencing other major mental health issues, call a psychologist, psychiatrist, or other mental health professional. If you're experiencing a psychiatric or medical emergency, call 911 or go to your nearest emergency room.

In sum, integration has become the standard approach in CBT, and it is exactly the approach we will take in this workbook. We'll work to understand how thoughts, feeling, and behaviors are related. A diagram of these elements looks like this:

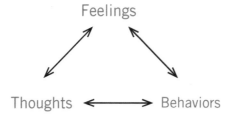

Each element affects both of the others. For example, when we feel anxious, we tend to have thoughts of danger and want to avoid the thing we fear. Additionally, when we think something is dangerous we fear it (feeling) and want to avoid it (behavior). Consider the figure below, which Ted completed with his therapist.

Situation: Trying to cross a bridge while hiking

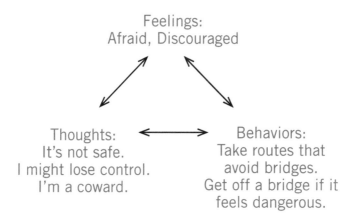

Think of a recent situation where you felt a strong emotion, perhaps anxiety or sadness. Briefly describe the situation in the space below.

_____

_____

_____

_____

_____

_____

Using the diagram below, write down the feelings you had, the thoughts you can remember having, and what you did.

What I felt:

_____

_____

_____

_____

What I thought: What I did:

_____   _____

_____   _____

_____   _____

_____   _____

_____   _____

_____   _____

Do you notice any connections among your feelings, thoughts, and actions? Use arrows to draw these connections in the diagram. We'll return to this model of connections many times throughout this book. But first, let's take a closer look at the guiding principles that give CBT its particular feel and make it highly effective.

The Principles of CBT

CBT is like other therapies in many ways. For one, it involves a supportive relationship between therapist and client. Effective CBT therapists have positive regard for their clients and strive to understand how they see the world. As with any successful therapy, CBT is a deeply human endeavor. At the same time, CBT has its own distinctive approach. Here are some of the main principles that define CBT:

CBT IS TIME LIMITED

When treatment is open-ended, we can tell ourselves, "I can always work on that next week." However, CBT is designed to provide the maximum benefit in the shortest possible time—generally around 10 to 15 sessions—which minimizes human suffering as well as cost. A shorter course of treatment can also motivate us to focus our efforts on getting the most out of it.

CBT IS EVIDENCE BASED

CBT therapists rely on techniques that have been well tested in research studies. Based on these studies, therapists can estimate how long treatment will take for a given condition and how likely a person is to benefit. CBT therapists also gather data during treatment to see what is and isn't working so they can adjust accordingly.

CBT IS GOAL ORIENTED

CBT is all about moving toward *your* goals. You should have a good sense of whether the treatment is addressing your goals, and how much progress you're making toward them.

CBT IS COLLABORATIVE

It can be easy to think of a CBT therapist as the one who does the "fixing." This view matches our typical model of seeking help—for example, a surgeon performs surgery to fix your bum knee. But CBT can't be done *to* a person. Instead, the therapist is an expert on CBT, and clients have specialized knowledge about themselves. Success in CBT requires bringing together these perspectives to tailor a treatment to the client's needs. In the same way, you and I will collaborate through this workbook: I'll provide the CBT techniques, and you'll customize them to fit your goals.

IS THAT CBT?

CBT is an umbrella term for many specific types of therapy. Some powerful CBT programs don't have "CBT" in their name. A few examples include:

- **Exposure and Response Prevention** for obsessive-compulsive disorder (OCD)
- **Prolonged Exposure** for post-traumatic stress disorder (PTSD)
- **Dialectical Behavior Therapy** for borderline personality disorder
- **Panic Control Therapy** for panic disorder

Each of these therapy programs adapts the basic ingredients of CBT to address the condition it's designed for. So if you're looking for CBT, know that it might not be called CBT.

On the flip side, not everything that's called CBT actually is. If you seek out a CBT therapist, make sure he or she has specialized training in this approach. The Resources section at the back of the book includes a link to guidelines for finding a CBT therapist.

CBT IS STRUCTURED

With CBT, you should expect to have a good idea of where you're heading and how to get there. CBT begins with setting clear goals and then designing a roadmap-like treatment plan. Once we have the map, we'll know if we're moving toward our goals. The structure of CBT builds on itself, with earlier sessions laying the foundation for later ones. For example, in week 3 of this program we'll talk about how to identify unhelpful thoughts, and in week 4 we'll work on how to change those thoughts.

CBT IS FOCUSED ON THE PRESENT

Compared to other therapies, CBT spends more time dealing with what's going on now than on past events. This is not to say that CBT therapists ignore the past or treat childhood events as irrelevant. Rather, the emphasis is on how to change current thoughts and behavior to bring about lasting relief as quickly as possible.

WHAT ABOUT MEDICATION?

Many people choose to take medication to treat their anxiety and depression, with or without psychotherapy. Selective serotonin reuptake inhibitors (SSRIs) like fluoxetine (Prozac) and sertraline (Zoloft) are the most commonly prescribed for depression, and they are also prescribed for anxiety. Other medications are often prescribed for anxiety, especially benzodiazepines like clonazepam (Klonopin).

Research trials have found that some medications can actually be as effective as CBT, at least as long as the medications are taken. Studies with follow-up periods tend to find that CBT does a better job protecting against relapse. For example, a 2005 study by Hollon and colleagues found that having CBT versus antidepressant medication lowered the risk of depression returning by 85 percent.

A person interested in psychiatric medication should consult a physician with extensive experience treating the person's condition.

CBT IS AN ACTIVE TREATMENT

This is a "roll your sleeves up" kind of treatment, with treatment emphasizing tackling clearly defined goals head-on. Both therapist and client are actively engaged in the process.

CBT IS SKILLS ORIENTED

Through CBT we learn techniques to manage the issues we're dealing with, practice them on our own, and take them with us when treatment is over. People in CBT often say things like, "I'm starting to recognize the tricks my mind plays on itself," "I can now test whether my thoughts are actually true," and "I'm getting better at leaning into my anxiety."

CBT EMPHASIZES PRACTICE

In most cases, therapy is one hour a week. That leaves 167 hours a week away from the therapist. And so a person must practice new skills between sessions to get the most benefit from them. Many studies have shown that people who do more work between sessions do better in CBT.

So far we've covered the basics of CBT and where it came from. In the past few decades, researchers have tested CBT treatments in clinical trials. Let's see what they've found.

How Well Does CBT Work?

Hundreds of research trials have tested the effectiveness of CBT for a wide range of problems. Fortunately, we don't have to read all of the studies to get the take-home message. Researchers can combine similar studies into a single study using sophisticated statistics in what is known as a meta-analysis.

Meta-analyses consistently find CBT has strong effects in treating anxiety, depression, and other conditions. And these effects are above and beyond any improvement we'd expect simply from the passage of time, because they were found in studies that included a waiting list control condition. For example, if 60 people signed up for a treatment study, half would receive an immediate 10 weeks of treatment while the other half would have their treatment delayed by 10 weeks. The study team could then compare the groups' symptoms after the first 10 weeks.

Researchers also study whether CBT is actually helpful, or if people get better just because they think they're receiving an effective treatment. To answer this question, scientists use a pill placebo—a pill that doesn't contain any actual medicine—which controls for any expectation a person might have for improvement simply because the patient thinks they are getting treatment. CBT treatments for many conditions are far superior to a pill placebo.

How does CBT stack up against other psychotherapies? The vast majority of programs with strong support for their effectiveness are CBT in nature. For example, only CBT has strong research support in the treatment of panic disorder, adult attention deficit/hyperactivity disorder (ADHD), phobias, and obsessive-compulsive disorder. While some other kinds of psychotherapy are also effective, there is evidence that CBT is significantly more effective than less structured and more open-ended treatments. Part of the evidence base for CBT programs is driven by the fact that they are relatively easy to standardize and test in research studies, compared to more free-form therapies.

The fact that CBT programs are straightforward also makes them well suited to export from the therapy office into self-directed treatment, like this workbook and Internet-based CBT. Meta-analyses consistently find that self-directed CBT can reduce symptoms of anxiety and depression.

While the self-directed treatments are effective by themselves, studies also find that some people benefit even more from "guided self-help" (limited involvement from an expert, whether by phone, mail, e-mail, or in person). For these reasons, this book was designed to be used alone or with the guidance of a professional.

In the next section, we'll look at why CBT programs work so well. Before we do, take a few moments to think about a time you tried to make a specific change in your life. For example, maybe you wanted to exercise more or learn something new.

Change I wanted to make:

_____

_____

_____

_____

_____

_____

Now write down (1) what went well, (2) what didn't go well, and (3) any obstacles you ran into:

_____

_____

_____

_____

_____

_____

_____

Why CBT Works

CBT is based on a few basic principles about the relationships among thoughts, feelings, and behavior. While CBT has been recognized as a treatment method for only a few decades, the principles it rests on are hardly new. For example, as the Greek philosopher Epictetus wrote nearly 2,000 years ago, "People are not disturbed by things but by the view they take of them." Aaron Beck and Albert Ellis said essentially the same thing in their writings.

So what does CBT add to the basic tenets that have been around for hundreds or thousands of years?

TARGETED EXERCISES

When we're feeling anxious or depressed, many areas in our lives might feel out of control. It can be hard to know where to begin to focus our energies. CBT introduces structure that gives us an idea where to start. Rather than try to tackle everything at once, a typical session in CBT will focus on one or two specific issues. Having targeted exercises to practice between sessions further focuses our efforts.

PRACTICE EFFECTS

Most of the time, we flourish not by learning new things but by acting on what we already know. Knowing the principles of CBT is essential, and *practicing* them is what drives their effectiveness. It's the same as for an exercise program: Knowledge about the benefits of physical activity is helpful, but we only benefit from actually exercising. CBT serves as a steady reminder of the plan to follow toward our goals.

BREAKING LOOPS

When we're highly anxious or depressed, our thoughts, feelings, and behaviors tend to work against us in a vicious spiral. CBT helps us break out of this spiral. As we practice better thinking and more helpful behavior, our thoughts and actions reinforce each other in a positive direction.

SKILLS ACQUISITION

Finally, the focus on learning and practicing new skills in CBT ensures we take the treatment with us once it's over. When we face new challenges, we're armed with a set of tools for dealing with them. So the benefits of CBT far outlast the treatment.

In this chapter, we covered a brief history of CBT as well as its basic principles and why it works. Now, take a few moments to check in with yourself and see how you can apply what you've learned in your own life. Write your thoughts and feelings, taking care to be as open as possible. Invest some time here. Resist the urge to skip this step and jump ahead to the next chapter. Once you're finished, we'll continue working toward the seven-week plan in chapter 2.

_____

_____

_____

_____

_____

_____

_____

_____

_____

_____

_____

_____

_____

_____

_____

_____

_____

_____

_____

_____

_____

_____

Chapter Check-In

CHAPTER TWO

Understanding Anxiety and Depression

In the previous chapter, we reviewed how and why CBT was developed and the basics of how it's used to treat anxiety and depression. We considered some of the ways that CBT is unique—for example, CBT is highly structured and focuses on practicing key skills.

In this chapter, we'll cover exactly what anxiety and depression are, as well as how they can disrupt our lives. First, let's start with anxiety.

Mel's Dog Phobia

"What is it, Mommy?" Mel's daughter asks as she feels her mom's hand tense around her own. The young girl can sense something's wrong.

"It's okay, sweetheart," Mel replies, trying to sound casual. "Let's just cross the street." What she doesn't tell her four-year-old daughter is that she desperately wants to avoid the dog she spotted farther down the sidewalk.

Ever since she was chased by a big dog that got out of its yard, Mel has been terrified that dogs will attack her. Although she wasn't hurt, she's certain she would have been if the owner hadn't called off his dog. Now, when she sees a dog, her heart pounds, she breaks into a sweat, and she avoids them if possible.

All the elements of a CBT framework are here. First, Mel believes that dogs are extremely dangerous. Given that belief, it's no wonder that she feels fear whenever she sees one. She experiences:

See Dog → Feel Afraid

With our CBT understanding, we can add the intervening thought:

See Dog → "Dogs are dangerous" → Feel Afraid

Second, she avoids dogs. By avoiding them she gets some relief from her fear. In some sense, her avoidance is working, at least in the short term. Unfortunately, it also makes her more likely to run from dogs in the future.

By avoiding dogs, Mel *never gets to learn what would actually happen if she approached one.* Therefore, her avoidance behavior *reinforces* her belief that dogs are dangerous.

To complete the loop, her fear affects her behavior, compelling her to avoid dogs. The fear she feels also strengthens her belief that dogs are dangerous— "Why else would I be so afraid of them?"

When Mel came for treatment of her fear of dogs, she was locked in a vicious spiral of thoughts, behaviors, and emotions, depicted in the diagram we've seen before:

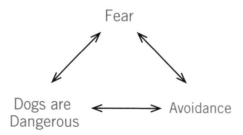

Let's see how CBT helped her to break free.

THOUGHTS

With her therapist's help, Mel identified her beliefs about dogs and what they were based on. Mel believed that dogs were pretty likely to attack—she estimated a 25 percent probability. Her therapist encouraged her to think about all the times she had been around a dog and how many times she or someone else had been attacked. Mel realized that out of thousands of encounters with dogs, she had been chased once.

> *"But still," she said, "it only takes once." Mel and the therapist then explored what had happened when she was chased. The dog may have just wanted to play with her—at least, that's what the owner had explained apologetically. But Mel still had been left with the feeling, "What if . . . ?"*

It's important to note that *simply changing her thoughts did not get rid of her extreme fear*. She felt only slightly less terrified around dogs. (You may be able to relate to this experience—for example, most people who have a phobia of flying know that it's the safest way to travel.) But she was now in a place where she was *willing* to face her fear, given the seemingly low risk involved.

BEHAVIOR

Next, Mel and her therapist made a list of ways she could practice being around dogs until she felt comfortable again—a process called exposure. They came up with fairly easy ones—staying on the sidewalk when a dog passed on the other side of the street—and ones that would be more challenging. At the top of her hierarchy was petting a big, "scary" dog like a German Shepherd or Rottweiler, assuming the owner gave permission.

The first few exercises weren't too bad, and Mel quickly got comfortable being in the vicinity of dogs. As Edna Foa and other psychologists have discussed, Mel's direct experience of not being attacked by the dogs had a powerful effect on her belief about dogs being dangerous. As she became less afraid, she had an easier time doing her harder exposures. Now her thoughts, behaviors, and feelings were working together *for her* rather than against her.

By the end of treatment, Mel could hardly believe how far she'd come in just a few sessions. She felt proud of herself for having faced her fears. She even surprised the therapist by getting a small dog. Through being around dogs in therapy, she realized she loved them. She's still appropriately cautious around dogs she doesn't know, but she no longer fears or avoids them.

The Faces of Anxiety

Anxiety can be useful. Think about all the ways anxiety helps us take care of our responsibilities. Without anxiety, we might not get out of bed in the morning. I'd probably be watching TV or surfing the Web if I didn't have some anxiety about my deadline to finish this book.

In many situations, we would think it was strange if a person didn't seem at least a little anxious, like during a first date or job interview. We might think the person didn't care.

ANXIETY BY THE NUMBERS

Anxiety disorders are the most common psychiatric conditions that people experience. How likely are people to have a major type of anxiety at some point?

- **Eighteen percent** will have a **specific phobia**.
- **Thirteen percent** will have **social anxiety disorder**.
- **Nine percent** will have **generalized anxiety disorder**.
- **Seven percent** will have **panic disorder**.
- **Four percent** will have **agoraphobia**.

Women are about 70 percent more likely to have an anxiety disorder than men. The gender difference was greatest for specific phobias and least for social anxiety disorder.

Anxiety also protects us from danger and prompts us to protect the people we care about—for example, making parents keep an eye on their kids near a swimming pool. In short, anxiety helps us survive, be productive, and get our genes into the next generation.

So when is anxiety a disorder? Mental health professionals in the United States generally use the fifth edition of the American Psychiatric Association's *Diagnostic and Statistical Manual of Mental Disorders*—abbreviated *DSM-5*—to determine when a psychiatric diagnosis is warranted. The *DSM-5* notes that an anxiety disorder may be present when:

- **The anxiety is overblown compared to the actual danger**. Being very afraid when we find a black widow spider is less likely to be a disorder than is being terrified of houseflies.
- **The anxiety consistently appears in certain situations, and for a period of weeks or months**. The *DSM-5* includes lengths of time that anxiety must be present before any diagnosis is likely. For example, symptoms of panic disorder must last at least a month to be diagnosed, while symptoms of generalized anxiety disorder must be present for at least six months.
- **The person is really upset by the anxiety**, rather than being able to shrug it off and move on.
- **The anxiety gets in the way of a person's normal activities**. For example, Mel's fear and avoidance of dogs was making it hard for her to do regular activities outside of her home.

Now, let's review the main types of anxiety that adults experience, according to the *DSM-5*.

SPECIFIC PHOBIA

Specific phobia involves excessive anxiety and strong, often irrational fear of a given object or scenario. People can have phobias about virtually anything—from spiders to injections to clowns. The *DSM-5* notes that certain fears are more common, including animals, certain "natural environments" like heights and storms, and situations like flying or riding in elevators. Sometimes a bad experience led to the fear (as with Mel's fear of dogs), but many times we can't identify a cause. If you've dealt with a specific phobia, you know how upsetting it can be, and how strong the drive is to avoid what you fear.

SOCIAL ANXIETY DISORDER

Social anxiety disorder involves a strong fear of social scenarios. While it might seem like a specific phobia of social situations, it is different from phobias in important ways. First, the fear is ultimately of embarrassment. It seems almost cruel that oftentimes the fear is that "I'll look anxious," which only leads to more anxiety.

Also, with phobias we usually know if the thing we're afraid of happened. For example, we know if we fell from a great height or if the elevator got stuck. Social anxiety disorder, on the other hand, involves *guesses* about what others are thinking: "Do they think I sound dumb?" "Am I making him feel awkward?" "Are they bored?" Even when people say nice things to us—"Great job on your talk today"—we might not believe them. We might be left believing that our performance was terrible, even though nothing clearly bad happened.

PANIC DISORDER

People with panic disorder are often struck by bouts of fear, seemingly out of nowhere, with clear and sudden onset. As unpleasant as they are, panic attacks *per se* are not a disorder; only about one in six people who have had a panic attack (see sidebar) actually have panic disorder. The attacks have to happen

THE EFFECTS OF PANIC

A panic attack is not subtle—it's like an alarm going off, and it gets our attention. During panic, the body's sympathetic nervous system launches a "fight or flight" response, releasing chemicals like adrenaline that prepare us to deal with danger. Here are the common effects of this fight-or-fight alarm, drawn in part from a workbook by panic experts Michelle Craske and David Barlow:

- The heart beats faster and stronger.
- We breathe faster and deeper, which can lead to strange sensations like dizziness or feeling light-headed. It can also lead to derealization—what some describe as a feeling that reality is "bending"—or depersonalization, which is a feeling that you're not connected to your body.
- We sweat more, which can fuel self-consciousness.
- Our digestive systems are affected, which can cause nausea or diarrhea.
- The muscles tense to prepare for action, which can cause trembling.
- We probably have an overwhelming desire to get out of the situation we're in.
- When an alarm goes off, we try to figure out what's wrong. If there's no obvious explanation, as Craske and Barlow point out, the mind is likely to think there's something wrong *internally*—that I'm having a medical emergency, like a heart attack or stroke, or am about to "lose control." These fears only intensify the alarm signal.
- Once the attack is winding down, we'll probably feel exhausted from the stress and strain of the panic. We may cry as activity increases in the parasympathetic nervous system (which calms us down).

repeatedly and be unexpected, and a person has to either worry about having more attacks or change their behavior—for example, avoiding driving at certain times of day. The urge to avoid places where panic is likely to happen can be so strong that it leads to a condition called agoraphobia.

AGORAPHOBIA

While it sounds like a kind of specific phobia, agoraphobia is really about avoiding places where we think *it would be really bad to panic* (or do something else embarrassing, like have uncontrollable diarrhea). According to the *DSM-5*, a person with agoraphobia is likely to avoid things like public transportation, bridges, movie theaters, lines at the grocery store, or just being out and about without a "safe" companion who could help if something happened. In some cases, the anxiety and avoidance are so strong that a person will stop going out of the house at all, sometimes for years.

GENERALIZED ANXIETY DISORDER (GAD)

Persistent and pervasive worry is the hallmark of generalized anxiety disorder. In addition to excessive and hard-to-control worry, things like trouble sleeping, difficulty concentrating, and feeling tired all the time are part of GAD. While panic represents the threat of immediate danger, GAD is on the opposite end of the spectrum. The anxiety is spread over multiple areas (thus "generalized") and is experienced as a grinding dread about all kinds of "what ifs." As soon as one worry is resolved, another takes its place.

Do you suffer from a particular form of anxiety? The following checklist may help give you a sense of what kind(s) of anxiety you might have, if any.

THE ANXIETY CHECKLIST

Place a mark next to the statements that describe you.

CATEGORY A

☐ A certain situation or thing (for example, heights, blood, snakes, flying on an airplane) almost always causes me tremendous fear.

☐ If at all possible, I avoid the situation or thing I'm afraid of.

☐ When I can't avoid my feared situation or thing, I feel intensely uncomfortable.

☐ My fear is probably more intense than makes sense, given the actual danger.

☐ I've had this intense fear for at least several months.

CATEGORY B

☐ I've had more than one abrupt spell of intense fear.

☐ During these spells my heart raced or pounded, I was sweating, I felt nauseated, and/or I was shaking.

☐ During these spells I felt short of breath, had chills or hot flashes, felt lightheaded, and/or felt separate from my body.

☐ I've worried about what these spells are and if I'll have more of them.

☐ I've tried to avoid anything that might trigger another spell of intense fear.

CATEGORY C

☐ I generally feel intense anxiety about using public transportation and/or being in open spaces like a parking lot.

☐ I generally feel intense anxiety when I'm in enclosed places (e.g., a movie theater), being in a crowd, waiting in line, and/or going out of the house alone.

☐ I worry that I might have a hard time escaping these situations if I had a panic attack or some other crisis.

☐ When I can, I avoid these situations, or try to get someone I trust to go with me.

☐ The fear I feel is probably greater than the actual danger in these situations.

☐ I've been afraid of these situations for at least several months.

CATEGORY D

☐ I feel very anxious in situations where I think I may be judged or criticized. Examples include public speaking, meeting new people, or eating in public.

☐ I'm afraid that I'll be publicly humiliated and/or rejected by others.

☐ I avoid social situations whenever I can.

☐ If I can't avoid a social situation, I feel intensely uncomfortable.

☐ My social fears are probably excessive in light of the actual threat.

☐ I've had intense anxiety about social settings for at least several months.

CATEGORY E

☐ I worry excessively about many things most days.

☐ It's hard to stop worrying once I start.

☐ When I'm worrying a lot I feel tense, irritable, restless, and/or easily fatigued.

☐ Worrying makes it harder to concentrate and/or disturbs my sleep.

☐ I've been a "worrier" for at least six months, and maybe most of my adult life.

Do your symptoms cluster in one or more specific categories? The categories are:

☐ **A:** Specific Phobia

☐ **B:** Panic Disorder

☐ **C:** Agoraphobia

☐ **D:** Social Anxiety Disorder

☐ **E:** Generalized Anxiety Disorder

Whatever category your symptoms might fall in, this workbook provides tools that apply. You can find more suggestions for tools to address the specific condition you might be experiencing in the Resources section at the back of the book.

You can find a copy of this checklist online at callistomediabooks.com/cbt.

Zeroing in on Depression

"What's the point?" Bill thinks to himself as his alarm clock goes off again. He realizes he definitely shouldn't hit snooze again if he's going to get to work on time. But he wants nothing more than to turn off the alarm, tell his boss he's not feeling well again, and stay in bed all day.

With a heavy sigh, he swings his legs around and onto the floor and sits with his head in his hands, trying to muster the energy to stand up.

Bill feels like he's moving through mud as he walks to the bathroom. He used to enjoy his morning shower—now it's all he can do to get in and wash up. For breakfast he manages to drink a small glass of orange juice; he looks at the boxes of cereal in his cabinet and closes the door.

He doesn't dare sit, knowing how hard it will be to get up again. Besides, his leg still hurts when he goes from sitting to standing. Three months ago, Bill broke his right tibia while trail running. For years, he would run with his friends several times a week, enjoying the outdoors and camaraderie. Now he can only ride the stationary bike at the gym as he heals.

As he drives to work, his leg hurts every time he presses the brakes. He curses himself for "being so stupid" as to break his leg. His mind wanders to other times he feels like he messed up—when he missed the last-second shot that would have tied the championship basketball game in high school; the unenthusiastic performance report he got at work last year; even the time he wet the bed at a seventh-grade sleepover. It all seems pathetic. He sighs as he parks his car and heads in for another day's slog at work.

Bill is caught in an episode of depression. It started with his injury, which led to losing many things he loves: conquering a difficult run, time with good friends, being outside. Many of the things that keep him feeling well were suddenly missing. As his mood dropped, he started to believe bad things about himself: that he's "pathetic" and "worthless."

DEPRESSION BY THE NUMBERS

- Depression is the **number one cause of disability**, according to the World Health Organization.
- About **350 million people** worldwide are depressed.
- As many as **25 percent of people in the United States** will experience major depression in their lifetime.
- As with anxiety disorders, **women** have about a **70 percent greater risk** for depression compared to men.
- **Younger generations** are more likely to experience depression than are their ancestors.

There are multiple ways CBT can interrupt the tailspin Bill is in. One of the most important is to find ways to replace the sources of joy and accomplishment that are now missing. In CBT, Bill will also take a close look at what he's telling himself, and he will see whether his thoughts make sense. Is he truly pathetic? Does breaking his leg mean he's stupid? The losses Bill experienced would take a toll on anyone, but they don't mean he has to stay depressed.

General Types of Depression

Depression takes many forms. Sometimes we don't even realize we're depressed when the condition is different from our idea of it. The *DSM-5* separates the broad category of depression into several specific types. Let's look at some of the subtypes.

MAJOR DEPRESSIVE DISORDER

The most common form of depression is major depressive disorder. It's what we usually mean when we say someone is "clinically depressed" or has "major depression." A person has to either feel down for most of the day *or* lose interest in almost all activities for at least two weeks. A person can be depressed but not actually feel "down." The average bout of major depression is about four months.

During the same two weeks, a person with depression will have other symptoms, such as sleeping a lot more or a lot less than usual, being much more or much less hungry, feeling exhausted, and having a hard time focusing or making decisions.

We also tend to feel bad about ourselves when we're depressed, either excessively guilty or completely worthless. Depression is a strong risk factor for suicidal thinking and even attempting suicide. Someone with major depressive disorder will probably feel like she's in mental pain and is likely to have a hard time doing normal activities.

Because there are nine symptoms of depression and five are needed for a major depression diagnosis, the condition can look quite different in different people.

PERSISTENT DEPRESSIVE DISORDER

Major depressive disorder tends to wax and wane, even without treatment. Within one year from when it begins, around 80 percent of individuals will have started to recover, according to the *DSM-5*. Others experience a more chronic form of depression called persistent depressive disorder. Consistent with the name, a person has to feel depressed most of the time for at least two years to receive this diagnosis. They will also have at least two other symptoms of depression, so the condition can be milder than major depressive disorder (which requires five symptoms). As the *DSM-5* makes clear, this is not to say that persistent depressive disorder is a "light" form of depression. Its negative effects can be at least as great as those of major depression.

PREMENSTRUAL DYSPHORIC DISORDER

A controversial diagnosis was added to the latest *DSM*: premenstrual dysphoric disorder, or PMDD. This form of depression occurs leading up to and during the first part of a woman's menstrual period. Contrary to some of the criticism of the diagnosis, it is not the same thing as premenstrual syndrome, or PMS. PMDD is to PMS what major depression is to feeling "depressed" when one's favorite team loses.

In addition to some of the symptoms of major depression, PMDD also includes symptoms like volatile mood swings, irritability, anxiety, feeling overwhelmed, and the physical symptoms associated with the premenstrual phase, like breast tenderness and feeling bloated. A woman must have these symptoms during most menstrual cycles to have the PMDD diagnosis. In a given year, around 1 to 2 percent of menstruating women will experience PMDD.

SPECIFIERS FOR DEPRESSIVE DISORDERS

Further complicating matters, each type of depression can have one of several "specifiers," or labels that tell us more about the nature of the depression. Here are some of those labels:

Single Episode versus Recurrent Episode. Some individuals only have a single episode of depression, whereas others have recovered and then have a recurrence of the condition.

Mild/Moderate/Severe. Depression can range from manageable to completely debilitating. The labels include:

- **Mild:** A person barely meets criteria for depression and is able to manage with the condition; this accounts for only about one in ten instances of major depressive disorder.
- **Moderate:** Major depressive disorder is classified as moderate in about two out of five instances, which by definition falls between Mild and Severe.
- **Severe:** Most depression symptoms are present and the person is miserable and unable to function well; the largest percentage of cases of major depressive disorder are classified as Severe, at around 50 percent.

With Anxious Distress. It might seem like anxiety and depression are opposites: anxiety is a high-energy state, depression a low-energy state. However, major depression is significantly correlated with every kind of anxiety diagnosis, meaning we're more likely to be anxious if we're depressed, and vice versa. The *DSM-5* includes a category of depression "with anxious distress," meaning that a person has at least two symptoms of anxiety or dread, e.g., feeling unusually restless, worrying that interferes with concentration, or fearing something awful might happen.

With Melancholic Features. Even when we're depressed, we often feel temporarily better when something good happens, like if we finish an important project

PHYSICAL MANIFESTATIONS OF DEPRESSION

Depression is best thought of as a whole-body illness. Physical manifestations of depression can include:

- **Changes in appetite:** People who are depressed commonly lose their appetite, often because food just doesn't taste as good. Others experience an *increased* appetite and may gain weight.
- **Trouble sleeping:** Sleep can change in either direction. Some people with depression have terrible insomnia, despite being exhausted; others sleep 12 hours a day and still want more sleep.
- **Physical agitation:** When a person is depressed, he might have a hard time sitting still and may constantly fidget, driven by an internal sense of unrest.
- **Being slowed down:** Some depressed individuals might move or talk slowly, to the point where other people might notice.
- **Slower healing:** Multiple studies have shown that we heal more slowly when we're depressed. For example, chronic wounds heal more slowly if we're depressed, and depressed patients recover more slowly from coronary bypass surgery.
- **Greater risk for dying from physical disease:** Among patients with coronary heart disease, for example, depression doubles the risk for dying.

Clearly depression is, quite literally, not just in a person's head.

or we spend time with loved ones. During severe depression, there can be a complete loss of pleasure in everything, even a person's favorite activities. A person with this kind of depression may have "melancholic features," which also include a worse mood in the morning, waking up in the morning at least two hours early, and consistent loss of appetite.

With Atypical Features. In contrast to melancholic features, atypical features include having a positive response when good things happen. Additionally, a person will have an *increased* appetite (and may gain weight) and *excessive* sleep, along with other symptoms.

With Peripartum Onset. No doubt you're heard of women experiencing "postpartum depression" after childbirth. The *DSM-5* states that about half the time, this form of depression actually starts before the baby is born. So depression around this period is called "peripartum," or "around delivery," rather than only after delivery. Depression with peripartum onset often includes severe anxiety. Three to six percent of mothers will experience depression with peripartum onset.

With Seasonal Pattern. Sometimes depression varies with the seasons, most often with a worse mood in the fall and winter as the days get shorter and mood improvement in the spring. This pattern is especially common among younger people and at higher latitudes—in Boston versus North Carolina, for example.

If you think you might be depressed, complete the following scale to see what symptoms of depression you're experiencing.

THE DEPRESSION SCALE

Over the past two weeks, how often have you been bothered by any of the following problems? Circle the number that matches your response for each item.

	Not at all	Several days	More than half the days	Nearly every day
1. Little interest or pleasure in doing things	0	1	2	3
2. Feeling down, depressed, or hopeless	0	1	2	3
3. Trouble falling or staying asleep, or sleeping too much	0	1	2	3
4. Feeling tired or having little energy	0	1	2	3
5. Poor appetite or overeating	0	1	2	3
6. Feeling bad about yourself, or that you are a failure or have let yourself or your family down	0	1	2	3
7. Trouble concentrating on things, such as reading the newspaper or watching television	0	1	2	3
8. Moving or speaking so slowly that other people could have noticed; or the opposite— being so fidgety or restless that you have been moving around a lot more than usual	0	1	2	3

Add up each column and write the totals here: ____ + _____ + _____ + _____

= **Total Score:** _____

Your total score provides an estimate of the degree of depression that you're experiencing:

0–4   Minimal
5–9   Mild
10–14   Moderate
15–19   Moderate to Severe
20–27   Severe

Depression can make it hard to focus on simple tasks, let alone taking on a workbook. If you're suffering from anything beyond mild to moderate depression, seek the services of a professional in addition to using this book.

You can find a copy of this form online at callistomediabooks.com/cbt.

In this chapter, we covered the many ways that we can experience anxiety: the specific fears in phobias, the terror of panic disorder, the avoidance with agoraphobia, the fear of humiliation in social anxiety disorder, and the never-ending worries of generalized anxiety disorder. We also covered the various forms of depression, including the most common, major depressive disorder.

The good news is that however anxiety and depression present themselves, a core set of CBT techniques can help control them. The first step in managing anxiety and depression is to have clear goals, which will be the topic of the next chapter.

For now, take some time to write down any reactions you have to this chapter. Which types of anxiety and/or depression could you identify with? Write down any other thoughts or feelings you're having at this point. In the next chapter, week 1, you'll identify your goals for this program.

PART TWO

SEVEN WEEKS

This rest of this book is organized around a seven-week plan that builds on itself week by week. First, we'll work to develop a solid treatment plan; then we'll focus on applying the skills of CBT.

Sometimes when we're starting a new program, we can be tempted to skip over certain parts, especially when we think we already know what will and won't work for us. Don't succumb to this temptation. I encourage you to do the full program, including each writing exercise. Interacting with the following material in multiple ways— reading, thinking, writing—will give you more opportunities to develop and follow the plan that will be most beneficial to you. You also won't have to wonder if you could have gotten more out of it when you get to the end; you'll know you did everything.

Setting Your Goals and Getting Started

In the previous chapter, we looked at the types of anxiety and depression people commonly experience. While it helps to have a system for diagnosing these conditions and understanding the symptoms, no two experiences of depression or anxiety are the same. Even people who have the same symptoms will experience them in different ways based on their unique histories, personalities, and life situations.

For this reason, we can't just take CBT off the shelf and say, "Here; do *this*." We have to understand your specific situation, and where anxiety and depression fit in the landscape of *your life*. Once we have a clear understanding of the challenges, we can figure out what changes you want to make. In other words, we have to know what your *goals* are. This chapter is all about determining your goals for this program.

"Here it comes," Phil says to himself, recognizing a familiar feeling from autumns past—the uneasiness, the low energy, the withdrawal. Already he's started skipping his morning workouts once or twice a week, and e-mails from his friends sit unanswered in his inbox.

His wife, Michelle, said something this morning as they ate breakfast: "Maybe you should see someone." He knows what she means—see a therapist. He's been reluctant to seek professional help in the past.

The next day, Phil talks to a good friend whose wife is a psychologist. His friend recommends someone his wife went to graduate school with who specializes in cognitive-behavioral therapy. He calls the psychologist and sets up a time to meet.

During their first meeting, Dr. Whitman talks with Phil about what brought him to treatment. Phil tells him about his seasonal pattern of low mood and anxiety. They discuss Phil's life: his family relationships, work, and friends, among other things. When Dr. Whitman asks what his goals are, Phil says, "I want to feel better this fall and winter."

Dr. Whitman works with Phil to flesh out what "feeling better" would look like. How would his life be different? Are there things he would be doing more? Phil thinks it over and comes up with some specific goals to focus on.

Dr. Whitman gives a brief overview of the treatment and how it can help Phil move toward his goals. He emphasizes that Phil has already done a lot of the work by seeking help and being specific about what he wants to change. Phil leaves the session with forms and instructions to monitor how he spends each day.

That night at dinner, Phil talks with Michelle about the session and says he's optimistic that the work will be helpful. As part of his homework, he and Michelle review his goals together, and Phil gets Michelle's input on some more specifics that he wants to work toward.

What Brought You In?

When I meet with someone for the first time in my clinical practice, I start by asking what brought them in for therapy. I'd encourage you to answer this question, as well. What compelled you to pick up this book? How long have you been dealing with these issues? How often do they come up? Why now—what made you decide that it was time to take action? You can be brief here; we'll get into more specifics later in the chapter.

_____

_____

_____

_____

_____

_____

_____

_____

Your Strengths

Whatever we might be struggling with, we are more than our struggles—we also have strengths that have kept us going, and they can get us through new challenges. Please take a moment to consider your own strengths. What are you good at? What do the people who know you best appreciate about you? Write your response in the space below. If you draw a blank, consider asking someone who cares about you what they see as your strengths.

_____

_____

_____

_____

_____

_____

_____

Taking Stock

I'd like you to think about how your life is going, including the ways anxiety and depression may be affecting things. I've chosen six areas that I routinely assess as a psychotherapist. We'll consider each of these areas in turn. Take your time. The work you're doing this week is as important as anything you'll do in this program.

RELATIONSHIPS

Relationships have a powerful effect on our well-being, for better and for worse. An unhappy marriage, for example, is a strong predictor of poor life satisfaction and is even associated with being suicidal. On the other hand, during the hardest times in our lives, even one supportive relationship can make the difference between being crushed and coming through strong. We'll consider family and friend relationships separately.

Family. *Phil has a strong relationship with his wife, although he finds that when he's depressed he isn't as present and is quicker to snap at her. He also doesn't have the energy to do enjoyable activities with her, like going out to dinner, getting away for the weekend, even being intimate. He realizes that a certain "spark" has been missing from their relationship.*

Think about how things are going in your family relationships, including your family of origin (parents, siblings) and, if applicable, the family you formed as an adult (partner, kids, in-laws, etc.).

Consider the following questions: What's going well in your relationships? Where do you struggle? Is your family going through any major stresses? Is there a family member who's having a hard time, and who might be affecting the whole family dynamic?

Are there family members you're missing, who have moved out of your life either through death or for other reasons? As much as you love your family members, do you crave more time alone?

You might also consider how your family relationships affect your anxiety and/or depression. Alternately, what effects have your anxiety/depression had on your family? Record your thoughts below.

_____

_____

_____

_____

_____

_____

_____

_____

_____

_____

_____

_____

_____

_____

_____

_____

_____

_____

_____

Friends. *In general, Phil is happy with his friendships. However, many of his good friends now have kids and have become less available. He misses how things used to be. As he heads into the fall, Phil spends less time with his friends. Each spring he comes up with excuses for why he's been out of touch. He can tell his friends are inviting him out less since they expect him to decline.*

People vary in how many friends they need—some of us are satisfied with one or two close friends, while others need a big social network.

Do you have a strong group of friends? Do you get to spend as much time with them as you'd like? For example, have friends moved away or have your relationships changed for other reasons? Have your anxiety and depression had an impact on your friendships? Record your thoughts below.

_____

_____

_____

_____

_____

_____

_____

BASIC HUMAN NEEDS

One way to think about our goals is to ask how much our psychological needs are being fulfilled. Countless studies have shown humans need three things:

- **Autonomy:** the ability to decide for ourselves what we do, without being overly controlled by others
- **Relatedness:** meaningful and satisfying connections to other people
- **Competence:** feeling like we're good at what we do and able to put our talents to use

The better these needs are met, the more life satisfaction we'll experience. For example, high satisfaction of our psychological needs is linked to lower shame, depression, and loneliness. Importantly, reaching our goals means more to us when these goals are in line with our basic psychological needs.

Consider the extent to which each of these needs is met in your own life as you formulate your goals.

EDUCATION AND CAREER

Phil's job involves support work for a financial firm. It's not terribly challenging, and the pay is good. He sees work mostly as a "necessary evil." He enjoys some of his colleagues, but for the most part experiences work as neutral to negative. Since he's been feeling down, he knows he hasn't been as effective at his job. He's slower to respond to calls and e-mails and calls out sick more often.

How are things for you in your work life, whether you work outside the home or your primary job is taking care of your children? Naturally, depression and anxiety affect our relationship with our work, so try to consider your job when you're feeling well. Do you love your work? Find it meaningful? Do you enjoy your coworkers? Are you overextended, constantly feeling like you don't have enough time to do everything well? Do you struggle with the demands of work and home? Or are you bored at work? Do you feel like you have abilities that aren't being put to use? Or maybe worst of all, are you bored *and* overtaxed?

Write your thoughts below. Include any effects that anxiety and depression have on your professional life. For example, it might be harder to concentrate and make decisions, or we may avoid work-related situations that make us anxious (like public speaking). We might even choose a career to minimize our anxiety. Also include any significant financial concerns.

_____

_____

_____

_____

_____

_____

_____

_____

FAITH/MEANING/EXPANSION

When Phil was younger, he felt like life had a purpose. He expected to do important things in his career and to make a meaningful contribution to others' welfare. Although he was never formally religious, he saw himself as part of an interconnected web of humanity.

Lately, though, Phil has felt less connected to humankind, and he misses a feeling of solidarity with others. As his anxiety and depression worsen, he feels cut off from other people and has a hard time connecting with anything outside himself.

What gives you a sense of purpose? As a general rule, we find purpose and meaning through connection to something larger than ourselves. Many of us find that connection through membership in a religious community. Perhaps we're inspired by sacred texts and by our belief in a divine being who cares about and communes with us.

Others among us find a sense of expansion—of extending our awareness and our connections—through the natural world or through a feeling of shared humanity with others. We may find our place in a vast universe through our identity as parents—as part of a continuing chain of breath and being that flows into the next generation.

At times, we may struggle to find a sense of identity and purpose. Maybe we've left the religion of our youth or suffered a major disappointment that calls into question so much that we held sacred.

Take some time to consider your own deepest source of meaning and purpose. What moves you? What are your passions? Do you experience enough beauty in your life? Do you have a clear sense of connection to what's most important to you?

_____

_____

_____

_____

_____

_____

_____

_____

_____

_____

_____

_____

_____

_____

_____

_____

_____

_____

_____

"There is nothing magic about change; it is hard work. If clients do not act in their own behalf, nothing happens."

—Gerard Egan, PhD, The Skilled Helper

PHYSICAL HEALTH

Dr. Whitman asks Phil several questions about his general health, his eating habits, how much physical activity he gets, and what substances (like alcohol) he regularly puts in his body. Phil makes connections between the state of his body and the state of his mind. When he exercises consistently, he feels mentally sharp and more optimistic. When he drinks too much or doesn't get enough sleep, his mood suffers. He also notices how feeling anxious and depressed can push him toward behaviors that make him feel worse.

There is greater recognition than ever before of the interdependence of the mind and the body, with the mind affecting the "machine" and vice versa. Take some time to think about your physical health.

General Health. Do you deal with any chronic health issues, like high blood pressure or diabetes? Do you worry about your physical health? What is your relationship with your body like?

_____

_____

_____

_____

_____

_____

_____

_____

_____

_____

_____

_____

_____

Physical Activity. Do you get regular physical activity that you enjoy, or does exercise feel like an unpleasant chore? Are there forms of movement you like, such as dancing or walking with friends, that don't feel like "exercising" at all?

_____

_____

_____

_____

_____

_____

_____

_____

_____

Drugs and Alcohol. What role does alcohol or other mood-altering substances play in your life? Have you had any problems with drug or alcohol use? Has anyone given you a hard time about it or told you to cut down?

_____

_____

_____

_____

_____

_____

_____

_____

_____

Food. Consider any issues you may have related to food. Do you routinely eat out of boredom or to change your mood? Do you ever struggle to eat enough, either because you're uninterested in food or you fear "getting fat"?

_____

_____

_____

_____

_____

_____

_____

_____

_____

_____

Sleep. Poor sleep makes everything more difficult. How have you been sleeping? Too much? Too little? Any problems falling asleep or staying asleep? Do you often wake up long before your alarm, unable to fall back asleep? Consider anything else that might affect your sleep—kids, pets, neighbors, a partner who snores, a demanding work schedule, etc.

_____

_____

_____

_____

_____

_____

_____

_____

_____

RECREATION/RELAXATION

When Phil feels well, he likes to do lots of things with his free time: read, go to sporting events, mountain bike, play with his dog. He's given up many activities in winters past, spending a lot of time instead reading "listicles" or watching videos on YouTube—things he doesn't even care about.

He talks with Dr. Whitman about the things he misses most. He feels stuck: On the one hand, he'd like to get back to his favorite activities. On the other, it's hard to find the energy and motivation.

We all need times when we can relax and unwind. Many things can crowd out our ability to have fun and "recharge": a demanding job, second jobs to make ends meet, health problems, the work of parenting—not to mention anxiety and depression.

What do you like to do in your free time? Are you constantly "on" or are there times when you can relax? Are there things you'd like to do more? Think about the last time you felt relaxed—what were you doing? Do you enjoy certain hobbies and pastimes? Or do your hobbies feel like a second job rather than restorative downtime? Do you find that, like Phil, you fritter away your free time on things that don't bring true enjoyment?

Have anxiety and depression affected your enjoyment of and participation in hobbies and pastimes?

_____

_____

_____

_____

_____

_____

_____

_____

_____

DOMESTIC RESPONSIBILITIES

"I'll get to it," Phil tells Michelle. He's been telling her for weeks that he'll orga-nize the garage. They've had to park the car in the driveway lately because the garage is in such disarray. He feels bad, but he doesn't have the energy or the motivation to begin.

All of us have responsibilities at home, which may include cleaning, buying and preparing food, paying bills, mowing the lawn, and taking out the trash. Are you able to take care of your daily responsibilities? Are there any issues between you and your partner or roommate(s) about how chores are divided? Write any relevant issues below.

If any other important issues weren't captured in the categories above, write them here.

Review

At this point, take some time to carefully re-read what you wrote for each life area. How do you feel as you read each section? Joyful? Overwhelmed? Anxious? Grateful? Underline the parts that stick out as the most important in each area. We'll return to these passages later.

What Are Your Goals?

We're now in a good place to start defining your specific goals. How do you want your life to be different at the end of these seven weeks, and beyond? For example, Phil developed the following list:

1 *Feel less anxious and depressed.*
2 *Go to work consistently.*
3 *Exercise regularly.*
4 *Spend more time with friends.*
5 *Have the energy and interest to be the spouse I want to be.*

Use the parts you underlined to guide your own goal development. In addition to how you want to *feel*, think of other ways you want your life to be different, including specific activities you want to be doing.

Remember, these goals are *yours*—not what you think someone else wants for you. They need to be things you value. There's no "right" number of goals, but somewhere between three and six goals usually works well. Write your goals in the Notes section at the end of this book, or on a separate sheet of paper.

Logging Your Time

In preparation for next week, we'll need a careful record of how you're spending your days. At the end of this chapter, you'll find the Daily Activities form. On the following page is a sample completed form. Each row is an hour. In the Activity column, simply write what you did during that time. Keep it short and simple. Obviously, our days aren't neatly divided into one-hour blocks, so just do your best.

You'll also record how much you enjoyed each activity and how important it was to you. Remember, the enjoyment and importance ratings are yours alone to make—nobody else gets to decide what you enjoy and find important.

Finally, you'll rate your overall mood for each day on a scale from 0 to 10, where 0 is very bad and 10 is very good.

Plan to fill out the form the same day you do the activities, either at the end of the day or throughout the day. If you wait until the next day or later, you'll forget important information.

DAILY ACTIVITIES

Today's Date: _Sat. 5/21/16_

TIME	ACTIVITY	ENJOYMENT (0–10)	IMPORTANCE (0–10)
8:00–9:00 AM	Sleep	–	8
9:00–10:00 AM	In bed awake	2	0
10:00–11:00 AM	In bed awake	2	0
11:00 AM–noon	Breakfast with Michelle	5	7
noon–1:00 PM	Reading listicles online	2	0
1:00–2:00 PM	Watching golf	4	3
2:00–3:00 PM	Watching golf	4	3

DAILY ACTIVITIES

Today's Date: _____

TIME	ACTIVITY	ENJOYMENT (0–10)	IMPORTANCE (0–10)
5:00–6:00 AM			
6:00–7:00 AM			
7:00–8:00 AM			
8:00–9:00 AM			
9:00–10:00 AM			
10:00–11:00 AM			
11:00 AM–noon			
noon–1:00 PM			
1:00–2:00 PM			
2:00–3:00 PM			
3:00–4:00 PM			
4:00–5:00 PM			
5:00–6:00 PM			
6:00–7:00 PM			
7:00–8:00 PM			
8:00–9:00 PM			
9:00–10:00 PM			
10:00–11:00 PM			
11:00 PM–midnight			
midnight–1:00 AM			
1:00–2:00 AM			
2:00–3:00 AM			
3:00–4:00 AM			
4:00–5:00 AM			

My Mood Rating for Today (0–10):_____

You can find a copy of this form online at callistomediabooks.com/cbt.

The work you've done this week has clarified how anxiety and depression are affecting your life and what changes you want to make. Throughout the rest of the program, you'll be setting small goals to help you move toward your larger, overall goals.

Review your goal list several times this week to see if you want to add anything. Take a moment to put reminders in your calendar, or put a copy of your goals somewhere you'll see it each day. It's easy to let a week go by without returning to this work.

Remember to complete the Daily Activities form for **four days** over the following week. You can download copies of it online at: callistomediabooks.com/cbt.

You can also plan now for when you'll tackle week 2, where we begin the work of moving toward your goals and getting back to life.

Take a few minutes to write down your thoughts, feelings, and any concerns you may have in the space below.

_____

_____

_____

_____

_____

_____

_____

_____

_____

_____

_____

ACTIVITY PLAN

1 Review your goal list several times.
2 Plan a specific time to do week 2.
3 Complete the Daily Activities form for four days.

Getting Back to Life

Last week, you did the crucial work of figuring out what changes you want to make. Over the past week your tasks were to review your treatment goals and to monitor how you're spending your time. Now it's time to put your plan into action.

"Maybe I should just get some ice cream," Kat says to herself as she ties her running shoes. Her motivation these days is already in the basement, and the summer heat makes a run even less appealing.

In January, Kat left a relationship she should have ended long before. She knows she made the right decision, but that doesn't make it any easier to be alone. She always thought she'd be married and have a family by her mid-thirties. Now she worries she may never find the right person, and that soon it will be too late for her to start a family.

She met Cal in the last year of her graduate program, and then followed him after she graduated three years ago. He had a good job offer in Boston, not far from where he grew up. She was from Seattle and happy to move with him and see a new part of the country. Cal's friends were now her friends, and Kat was happy to have a ready-made social network since it had never been easy for her to meet new people.

Their breakup was amicable, and their mutual friends all said they were glad they "didn't have to pick sides," because they were "really friends with both

Cal and Kat." Nevertheless, months later, Kat rarely heard from any of them and often saw social media posts of fun things Cal was doing with "their" friends. She felt less and less inclined to reach out to them herself. "They're probably glad they don't have to hang out with me anymore," she tells herself.

Kat realizes she doesn't feel like doing much of anything. She still goes to work, which is okay but not exactly her dream job, and she forces herself to run once a week. The only thing she looks forward to is eating ice cream and sitting in front of the TV. At least then she can tune out the vague unease she feels most of the time. For weeks she's been saying she's "in a funk," and today for the first time she acknowledges to herself: "I'm depressed."

We can see in Kat's situation many of the elements of anxiety and depression: Her mood is low most of the time, she's worried about her future, and she's starting to think more negatively about herself. Her activities bring her very little joy or satisfaction, and she has little motivation to do things she loves.

Many people who come to me for treatment describe life situations that resemble Kat's. In fact, their circumstances sound a lot like what we would create for someone *if we wanted to make her depressed*: high stress, low reward, and minimal engagement. When the little energy we have is spent doing things that are unrewarding, we continue to deplete ourselves mentally, emotionally, and spiritually.

In this program, as in many CBT programs, we'll start by getting ourselves to do more of the things we find rewarding—part of the "B" of CBT.

Why Start with Behavior?

CBT addresses both thoughts and behavior. We could start with either one, but most often CBT begins by addressing behavior. Why is that the case?

First, it tends to be the most straightforward place to begin. Doing more of the things we enjoy is not complicated. That's not to say it's *easy*, but it's relatively simple, and the simplest approach is generally the best place to start.

WHY AM I DEPRESSED?

We don't always know what caused our depression. Thankfully, we don't have to figure it out before we can start to feel better. In fact, studies by the late Susan Nolen-Hoeksema and her collaborators found that if we spend too much time trying to "get to the bottom" of why we're depressed, we can actually feel worse as our minds begin to ruminate unproductively. The fastest way to feeling better and staying better is *doing the things that keep us feeling well.*

Second, research has shown there's a big "bang for your buck" effect from getting more active. In other words, a little investment in behavior change can go a long way. Doing the right kinds of activities tends to have an antidepressant effect.

Finally, changing our behavior can "jump start" changes in our thinking. For example, we might believe, like Kat, that "nobody really wants to spend time with me." A quick way to test that belief is to ask our friends if they want to get together. When they (most likely) say "yes," we have evidence that people actually *do* like us enough to spend time with us.

The treatment approach we'll focus on in this chapter is called behavioral activation. While it's generally described as a treatment for depression, it can lower anxiety, as well.

What Should I Do?

Many things can lead to depression, such as losses (jobs, relationships) and major stresses. Whatever the cause, once we're feeling down, we tend to cut ourselves off even more from things that make us feel good. As a result, our mental, emotional, and physical resources are not replenished. Our "bank account," so to speak, is overdrawn.

When we do the right kinds of activities, we feel better. But what makes an activity "right"? The short answer is that it needs to be rewarding to you—it has to give you something you value. If we just said, "Do these things and you'll stop feeling depressed," we might be telling you to do things you don't care about. It's hard enough to do things we like to do when we're depressed and anxious, let alone activities we don't care about, or find aversive.

The developers of behavioral activation determined that the activities you plan have to come from your values, as described in a treatment manual by Carl Lejuez and his fellow authors. In this context, "values" doesn't have a moral or ethical overtone, although your values can include morality and ethics. Here, your values are anything that you enjoy, love, or get satisfaction from doing.

As with goals, you are the only person who can decide what your values are. The values you articulate here have to resonate with you. We often base our values on what we *think* should be important to us—maybe by relying on what our parents told us, or on what we think society expects of us. Instead, our values should be based on what brings us pleasure or enjoyment, gives us a sense of mastery or accomplishment, and feels like it's worthwhile.

And good news—you've already done a lot of thinking about these kinds of values through the work you did last week. Let's build on that work as you define your values.

WHICH COMES FIRST: DOING MORE OR FEELING BETTER?

When we're feeling down and stuck, we often become less active: We don't feel like socializing, exercising, taking care of our living space, and so forth. We can find ourselves stuck in a Catch-22: We won't feel better until we do more things, and we won't do more things until we feel better. We often tell ourselves that we'll be more active once we start feeling better. CBT takes the reverse approach, because we generally have more control over our actions than our feelings. If we wait till we feel well enough to be more active, we may be waiting a long time.

What's Important?

Kat has noticed her tendency to take "the path of least resistance" when faced with opportunities that would enrich her life. For example, some of her coworkers asked her to go out with them last Saturday night. Kat wanted to go and thought it would be fun to get to know her colleagues in a more informal setting. At the same time, she had some anxiety about the gathering: Would she have fun? Would she have interesting things to say? Would her coworkers think she was a stick in the mud? Her choices looked like this:

Kat's Choices

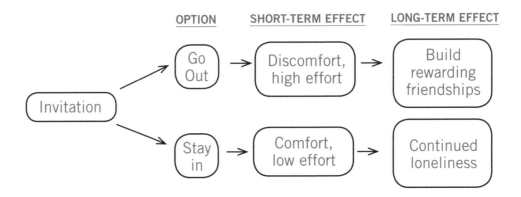

When Saturday night rolled around, Kat ended up texting her coworker to say she was "not feeling well" and couldn't make it. She watched TV with her cat and ate ice cream instead. That evening, she felt relieved. But on Monday morning, she felt lonely and ashamed when she heard her coworkers reliving the events from Saturday night. "I should've gone," she thought to herself.

Like Kat, we're often rewarded in the short term for doing things that aren't in our long-term interest. While staying in for the night felt better to Kat *that night*, it didn't move her toward her goals of being more active and expanding her social network. It also left her feeling bad about herself for not facing her fears.

How do we engineer activities that will stop the short-term reward we get from withdrawing, and increase our long-term reward by doing things we really care about?

There are three main steps:

1 Decide what you value in the areas we examined last week.
2 Come up with activities that fall under each of those values.
3 Plan and complete specific activities.

An example of a value and some corresponding activities might be:

Value: Beautifying my living situation.

- **Activity:** Weed the front garden bed.
- **Activity:** Plant flowers.
- **Activity:** Buy cut flowers.

In the next section, we'll look at clarifying our values.

VALUES

Notice, in the example above, that values have no endpoint. There's no time when we say we've "completed" beautifying our living situation. Values can extend through our entire lifetime. Activities, in contrast, are specific and have a beginning and an end, though they can be repeated as many times as we wish.

Using the Values and Activities form starting on the next page, write down some of your values under each life area. There are three spaces under each life area, and it's okay if you come up with more or fewer for each one. Keep in mind: Your values don't have to be "heavy" or dramatic. Anything that makes our lives better is a value. (For now, leave activities blank.)

VALUES & ACTIVITIES FORM

RELATIONSHIPS

Value: _____

    Activity: _____

    Activity: _____

    Activity: _____

Value: _____

    Activity: _____

    Activity: _____

    Activity: _____

EDUCATION/CAREER

Value: _____

    Activity: _____

    Activity: _____

    Activity: _____

Value: _____

    Activity: _____

    Activity: _____

    Activity: _____

FAITH/EXPANSION/MEANING

Value: _____

    Activity: _____

    Activity: _____

    Activity: _____

Value: _____

    Activity: _____

    Activity: _____

    Activity: _____

PHYSICAL HEALTH

Value: _____

    Activity: _____

    Activity: _____

    Activity: _____

Value: _____

    Activity: _____

    Activity: _____

    Activity: _____

RECREATION/RELAXATION

Value: _____

    Activity: _____

    Activity: _____

    Activity: _____

Value: _____

    Activity: _____

    Activity: _____

    Activity: _____

DOMESTIC RESPONSIBILITIES

Value: _____

    Activity: _____

    Activity: _____

    Activity: _____

Value: _____

    Activity: _____

    Activity: _____

    Activity: _____

You can find a copy of this form online at callistomediabooks.com/cbt.

Some of your values could fit under different areas. For example, "Spending time with friends" could be under Relationships or Recreation/Relaxation. When that's the case, pick the one that makes more sense for you; if you can't decide, just pick one at random. In the end, the important thing is coming up with and completing activities, not how we categorize them.

You probably won't finish identifying your values right now. Spend a few minutes thinking about each area, and come up with an initial list. You'll add to it later in the week.

ACTIVITIES

Now it's time to think about what activities fall under each value. These activities may be things that are both enjoyable and important—for example, going to a park with your family. Other activities might be high on enjoyment and low on importance, like watching a good movie. Many daily responsibilities are high on importance and don't provide a lot of enjoyment, like doing the dishes. These examples are for illustration purposes—you'll decide for yourself what's enjoyable and important.

"The key to a depression-free life is to develop healthier patterns of behavior where each day contains important and/or enjoyable activities that help you feel fulfilled and as if your life has a purpose."
—*Carl W. Lejuez et al., 2011, p. 123*

Activities that are low on both enjoyment and importance are, by definition, not ones that fit your values. As with values, the activities you choose don't have to be "epic." In fact, it's better if they're not—we don't need grand gestures when we're depressed and anxious, just small, simple steps. For example, Kat's completed list for Physical Health looked like this:

Kat's completed Values and Activities Form

PHYSICAL HEALTH

Value: _Enjoying good food_

   Activity: _Have a friend over for homemade ice cream_

   Activity: _Plan meals for the week_

   Activity: _Buy bread, cheese, and fruit and have lunch by the river_

Value: _Feeling fit and strong_

   Activity: _Get in bed by 10 pm_

   Activity: _Join a gym with a pool near my apartment_

   Activity: _Do high-intensity interval training with an online video_

Notice that Kat's activities are *specific* enough that she'll know when she's done them, as opposed to loosely defined goals like "get in shape" or "learn to cook." Activities that are too vague can feel unmanageable, which can lower our motivation to do them. Vaguely defined activities also don't give us a clear sense of when we've completed them; rather than having a sense of accomplishment, we foster the nagging feeling that "there's always more I could do." When we define clear and manageable activities, we're more likely to complete them and to feel good about having done them.

You don't have to come up with all new activities; definitely include ones you're doing already if you want to do them more often. These activities can provide a good starting point as you build more rewarding activities into your schedule. Also, don't feel pressure to completely finish your activity lists now. Take some time to brainstorm a few activities for each life domain. It's helpful to start the list and then come back to it later. You'll almost certainly have more ideas when you come back to it later in the week.

BINDING YOURSELF TO THE MAST

In Homer's epic poem *The Odyssey*, Ulysses wanted to hear the Sirens' song. However, anyone who heard the Sirens sing would be drawn in irresistibly, "warble[d] to death with the sweetness of their song." Obviously, Ulysses wasn't willing to die to hear their song. So, he had his men bind him to his ship's mast with ropes. He also had his crew plug their ears with wax so they wouldn't be able to hear the song. He instructed his men, "If I beg and pray you to set me free, then bind me more tightly still."

Ulysses looked ahead and saw a situation that would test him. He didn't trust his sheer willpower—he knew it wouldn't be enough when he was tested. Thus he put in place a plan that would prevent him from doing what he knew he must not do.

This metaphor is perfect for CBT. We often know in advance what's going to challenge us to abandon our intentions. Armed with this knowledge, we can arrange our lives in ways that make it harder to do things that aren't good for us. For example, having an exercise partner who's meeting us at the gym makes it less likely that we'll "bail" at the last minute when we feel like turning off the 5:30 a.m. alarm.

Look for opportunities in your own life to practice this approach, to increase the odds of doing what you want to do.

REVIEW DAILY ACTIVITIES FORM

With the principles of this week's activities in mind, spend some time reviewing your Daily Activities form from the past week. What do you notice? How often are you doing activities that feel enjoyable and important to you? Are there gaps during the day—times when you aren't doing much of anything? Or is the opposite the case—is practically every moment crammed with activity, with no time left to enjoy living?

Take a moment here to write down your observations and feelings about your recent activities:

_____

_____

_____

_____

_____

_____

_____

_____

_____

_____

_____

_____

WHERE TO BEGIN?

Now that you've made your list of values-based activities, we can figure out where to begin. Go through your list of activities and place a 1, 2, or 3 next to each activity, based on its difficulty. The easier activities will be a 1—things you're probably doing already or could do without much difficulty. An activity is a 3 if it's hard to imagine tackling just yet. To ones that fall somewhere in the middle, give a 2.

Like all of CBT, this part of the program will be progressive. You'll start by working your way through the 1s. For this week, pick three of the easiest activities that interest you the most. Usually it's best if they come from different life areas, to give yourself a variety of rewarding activities.

Write the activities you picked in the spaces below.

Activity 1:

_____

Activity 2:

_____

Activity 3:

_____

In the space to the left of each activity, write down which day you'll do it. Then, take a blank Daily Activities form and write the activity in the block of time when you plan to do it. Do the same thing for the other two activities, on a separate day (and form) for each one.

In the coming week, continue to monitor your daily activities on the days you have your specific activities planned.

RAISING THE ODDS

As you look at the activities you planned for this week, think carefully about what might get in the way of each one. While we can't guarantee we'll do the things we planned, we can push the odds in our favor.

One of the best ways to raise the odds is to make the activity manageable. Any small step in the right direction beats a big step not taken. For example, one of Kat's activities was to join a gym with a pool. She realized as she planned for it that this task felt overwhelming: "Which gym?" "Where are my goggles?" "I don't have a swimsuit I like"—and so forth. Kat made each of these obstacles—choosing a gym, finding goggles, and buying a swimsuit—its own activity. It's hard to over- state the value of momentum, so make the activities as small as necessary to get the ball rolling.

BENEFITS OF EXERCISE FOR ANXIETY AND DEPRESSION

Many studies have found that adding regular exercise into one's routine has a positive effect on both depression and anxiety. The effect is about the same size as that of antidepressant medication. Not surprisingly, the benefits diminish if a person stops exercising.

More intense exercise tends to be more beneficial, although it doesn't seem to matter whether the exercise is aerobic (e.g., running or cycling) or anaerobic (e.g., weights).

There are several explanations for why exercise might be beneficial for our psychological health:

- Exercise tends to improve sleep, and better sleep helps with pretty much everything.
- Exercise can distract us from negative thinking. When we're working hard physically, it's harder to focus on our problems.
- Exercise can lead to positive social contact if we're exercising with other people.
- Exercise can give us a sense of satisfaction from having done something good for ourselves.

Whatever the reason, regular exercise can be an important part of a treatment plan for depression and anxiety.

You can also benefit from carefully considering the "reward value" of each activity you plan. If an activity isn't enjoyable at the time, it needs to provide you with some satisfaction once it's done. Otherwise it's probably in the category of "not worth doing."

Whenever possible, plan a specific time to do the activity and protect that time. Without a time that's set aside, we can easily fall into the trap of "I'll do it later." When we can always do something tomorrow, we're less likely to do it today (or tomorrow).

Finally, aim to create accountability. Accountability can be as simple as telling someone we're going to do something, like saying to our spouse, "I'm going running in the morning." We'll know that if we don't go, we're likely to be asked about it. Keeping records of your activities during this program also helps you give an account—to yourself—of how you're doing.

To summarize, you're most likely to complete your planned activities when you:

1 Make each activity specific and manageable.
2 Make each activity enjoyable and/or important.
3 Plan a specific time for each activity.
4 Build accountability into your plan.

Add below any additional factors you know that are helpful to you; for example, focusing on one task at a time to prevent feeling overwhelmed.

_____

_____

_____

_____

_____

_____

_____

_____

_____

_____

_____

_____

_____

_____

Good work—you're now two weeks into this program. You've made your goals and have taken a big step in determining what activities will enhance your life. You divided your list of activities into easy, moderate, and hard, and chose three activities to do at specific times this week.

The goal of this program is to help you think and act in ways that move you toward your goals. In the next chapter, we'll begin identifying your thought patterns. Take a moment now to schedule time for week 3.

In the space below, reflect on what stands out to you from this week's work. What are the major takeaways? Was there anything that wasn't quite clear, which you'll need more time to think about? Note how you're feeling right now and as you look to the week ahead. I'll see you in week 3.

_____

_____

_____

_____

_____

_____

_____

_____

_____

_____

_____

_____

ACTIVITY PLAN

1 Complete your three activities at the scheduled times.
2 Continue to record your daily activities on the days of your scheduled activities.
3 Finish the Values and Activities forms you started.

Identifying Your Thought Patterns

In the previous chapter, you began to identify what you value in the major areas of your life as well as activities that support each of these values. You then chose three activities to complete. This week, we'll start by reviewing how your activities went, then turn to identifying your thought patterns.

Take a moment to review how your three activities went. What went well? What could have gone better? Write your thoughts in the notes section provided at the end of the book.

Activity 1:

Activity 2:

Activity 3:

What are your thoughts and feelings about planning and completing specific activities so far?

_____

_____

_____

_____

_____

_____

_____

_____

_____

_____

_____

_____

_____

A common response at this point in the program is: "I did my activities, but I didn't feel any better." If that happened for you, well done. That means you stuck to your plan. If you *did* get a lift from doing the things you planned, that's great. Either way, keep going.

This program is a lot like starting an exercise regimen—the first several workouts are going to be tough, and you won't feel a benefit right away. In the same way, adding a few activities is unlikely to make a big difference in the short term. If you keep at it, chances are you'll start to notice the difference.

As you did last week, choose activities to complete in the coming week. Last week, you planned three. This week, pick *four* activities. You can repeat an activity from last week if you need to revisit it, but try to add some new ones. It takes practice to find activities that strike a balance between challenging and manageable. Stick with ones that you gave a ranking of 1, unless you're confident you can complete a 2.

Write the activities in the spaces provided:

Activity 1:

_____

Activity 2:

_____

Activity 3:

_____

Activity 4:

_____

Keep in mind all the tips from last week as you plan your activities, including scheduling them into specific times in your week.

Identifying Thoughts with Neil

When Neil came to see me for the first time, he'd been out of work for six months. For 25 years he'd done in-house IT work for a large financial firm, and he'd been let go as the markets contracted and the company tightened its belt.

From the moment Neil was told to collect his things, he'd done everything right: He'd attended the outplacement service his firm paid for, he'd busied himself with networking and job applications—he'd made his employment search a full-time job. He was determined to treat being fired as an opportunity to find something better.

Still, nobody hired him, even though several interviews had gone well. As his unemployment dragged on, Neil's enthusiasm began to flag. It got harder to get an early start on his day, and he felt like he was just going through the motions of his job search.

Just before he called to schedule an initial visit, he received notice that his unemployment benefits would expire soon. Before the notice, he'd felt like he was hanging by a thread, and this last blow felt enormously stressful and depressing all at once. He was 52 years old and had financial commitments to his young adult children—to help his daughter, a recent college grad, pay her rent, and paying for his son's college tuition. With 10 years left to pay on his mortgage, the financial stress was overwhelming.

His wife was extremely supportive and good at encouraging him to do what he needed to do. At the same time, Neil knew he could lean on her only so much, since she had stresses and a full-time job of her own. He knew he was really struggling when he had a passing thought: "Maybe my wife and kids would be better off if I were dead so they'd get the life insurance money." He called me the same day.

Neil's positive traits were easy to appreciate. He was committed first and foremost to his family, and he couldn't stand the thought that he might not be able to provide for them as he always had. I could see that he strongly resisted the downward pull of his situation, trying to stay upbeat. But as my initial evaluation went on, I could see his defenses breaking down. When I asked him about his job search, he concluded by saying, with a half-smile, "I guess no one wants to hire an old man."

In the first couple of weeks of his treatment, Neil and I focused on getting him active again. His job search activities were a big part of his activity plan, of course, as was physical exercise and making time for enjoyable downtime (which he'd mostly given up because he didn't think he "deserved it"). As he worked through his activities, it became clear that powerful thoughts and assumptions were getting in his way. We would need to address his thinking head-on.

Review of Cognitive Approach

Many of our emotional reactions come from how we think about things that happen. As humans, we want to understand our world, so we create stories to explain events. For example, if a friend is upset with us, we might believe that this friend is prone to being irrational and has no real reason to be mad. If we believe that story, we might feel some irritation toward this friend. We could diagram the sequence like this:

Friend is upset with me →
"He's being irrational again." → Irritated at friend

What if you assume that your friend must be mad for a reason, and that it's your fault? You're likely to feel different emotions:

Friend is upset with me → "I'm a lousy friend." → Worried, guilty

A major challenge in understanding the thoughts that drive our own emotions is that they don't often announce themselves. Although we're bothered by our interpretation of an event, we *think* we're bothered by the event *per se*. What we usually experience is an event *causing* an emotion:

Friend is upset with me → Irritated at friend

or

Friend is upset with me → Worried, guilty

As a result, we don't have the opportunity to ask if the thoughts make sense, because *we don't even recognize that we had a thought*. It's hard to evaluate thoughts that we don't recognize as thoughts. For this reason, we need to practice recognizing our thoughts and beliefs. This practice is important enough that we'll devote the rest of this chapter to it.

You might notice some changes in your thought process simply from becoming more aware of what your mind is telling you. There's something about writing down our thoughts that can begin to change our relationship with them. When I notice that I'm *telling* myself things, I can see that those things may or may not be true.

How to Identify Thoughts

In an early session with Neil, he described a disappointing rejection from another company. When I asked him to talk more about what was disappointing, he replied, "It's just frustrating to still not have a job, y'know? I think anyone would be disappointed at this point."

Neil had a great point: It's not as though the things that were happening to him were positive events he was somehow twisting into negative events. It's inherently stressful to have financial responsibilities and be struggling to find work. At the same time, each of us responds differently to this experience. We needed to identify exactly what Neil's reactions were.

I asked Neil to relax and close his eyes, and to imagine where he was when he got the news that he hadn't gotten the job. Then I asked him to recount the conversation with the hiring manager—which he did—and I directed him to pay attention to how he felt. What emotions was he aware of? Did he notice any sensations in his body? Did any thoughts go through his mind?

Neil opened his eyes and said, "Yes. 'Why would anyone hire me?' That's the thought I had." I encouraged him to consider if there were an implicit answer to that question. "Well, I meant it rhetorically," he said. "What I meant was, nobody would hire me." As we continued talking, Neil told me that he saw himself as outmoded, "like a dinosaur." "I see all these recent college grads," he told me, "and they're my daughter's age, and we're interviewing for the same jobs. What hope does a gray-haired guy with bifocals have against these kids?"

Now it was easy to see what was so disappointing about this rejection—not only did he not get this job, but he told himself that there was something unchangeable about him (his age) that would prevent him from getting any job. He was telling himself things like "I shouldn't even waste my time. This is pointless." No wonder he was investing less in his job search, since it all seemed like wasted energy.

Take a few moments to think about a recent situation in which you felt a surge of unpleasant emotion. Think about where you were at the time and what was happening. Picture it as vividly as possible. Now briefly describe the event that led up to the change in mood. Also describe the emotion(s) you felt.

_____

_____

_____

_____

_____

_____

_____

Notice any thoughts you had at the time. Can you identify specific thoughts that could explain the resulting emotion? Write down your observations here:

_____

_____

_____

_____

_____

_____

_____

As you consider your own thoughts related to anxiety and depression, notice what time period the thoughts focus on. Some probably deal with explanations of things that have happened already. Others may be about future events—predictions of what could happen. Still others may be about what's happening right now. As you try to identify your thoughts, keep in mind that they could be about the past, present, or future.

Sometimes thoughts come as an image or an impression. Rather than thinking, "I'm weak," for example, we might have an image of ourselves as being small and powerless. When you're practicing identifying your thoughts, remember that they may or may not be in the form of words.

We can diagram the event, thoughts, and emotions from an episode. Neil's diagram for the recent job rejection looked like this:

Neil's Event/Thought/Emotion Diagram

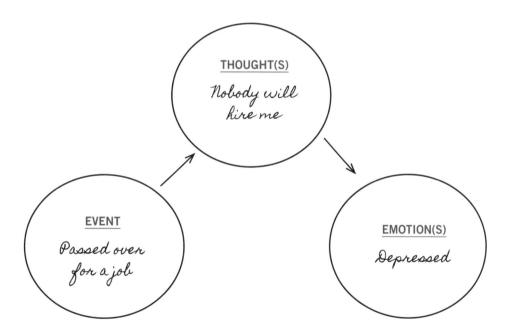

Think of a time when something happened in your own life that led you to feeling down or depressed. What thoughts went through your mind? Use the diagram below to illustrate this example:

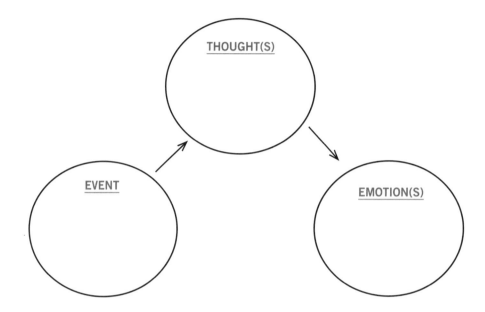

You can find a copy of this form online at callistomediabooks.com/cbt.

WHAT IF I CAN'T IDENTIFY A THOUGHT?

With other events that we looked at in retrospect, Neil didn't know what his thoughts were. "It's funny," he said, "but before we talked about these things I didn't even really think I was thinking. I just took the way I saw the world as fact. I'm still working on recognizing what my thoughts are." For these episodes, we left a placeholder—we would need to gather more information from new events to get a clearer understanding of his thinking.

A lot of times, it's hard to know exactly what we were thinking if we're not actually in the moment when we had the thought. If you weren't able to pinpoint a thought that led to an emotion, don't worry—you'll have plenty of opportunities to practice. In truth, learning to hear what we're telling ourselves is a skill we can refine throughout our lives. This is just the beginning.

One part of your activity plan for this week will be to record at least three instances when your mood dipped. You'll simply note what was happening, what you felt, and what thought(s) you had. You can record these episodes on the Identifying Thoughts form.

Common Themes in Anxiety and Depression

As Neil got to know his thoughts better, he recognized a familiar "cast of characters." Most of his disturbing thoughts were about his "hopeless" future, which he believed was a result of his old age and "obsolescence," which he took to mean he wouldn't be able to provide for his family, which he thought made him a worthless human being. No wonder Neil was depressed! He was constantly bombarded with thoughts about being old, unwanted, and useless.

As you record your own thoughts and emotions over the coming week, chances are you'll begin to notice recurring themes. It's like our mind is a jukebox and only has a few "hits" to play over and over when a triggering event "pushes the button." Our individual experiences of anxiety and depression will be closely related to the kinds of thoughts we often have.

Let's consider some common types of thoughts that come up in certain psychological conditions. We'll start with the anxiety disorders. You can skip the exercises for conditions that don't apply to you.

SPECIFIC PHOBIA

When we're afraid of something, we often believe it's dangerous. If we have a fear of flying, we might think mysterious noises on a plane indicate something's wrong. Two people might experience the same event in completely different ways, depending on their interpretation. When the plane's nose dips, you may be terrified if you think it means the engines have failed and the plane is going down fast. If you think, "Oh good; we've started our descent," you'll feel very different emotions.

Think about any of your own fears, and a recent time your fear was triggered. Are you aware of any thought that came up that may have contributed to your fear? Use the diagram below to record the event, the thoughts, and the emotions.

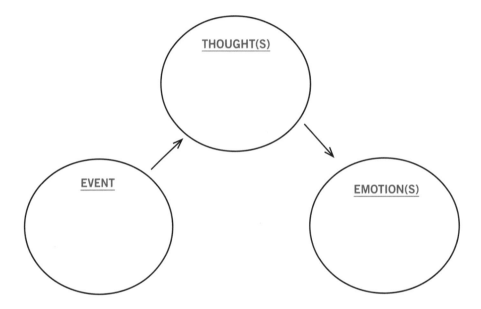

PANIC

Panic is fueled by beliefs that some horrible crisis is imminent if we don't escape from or change the situation *immediately*. I once had an episode of derealization in which my office felt strangely unfamiliar. I suddenly *knew* something was dreadfully wrong, and that I must be having a stroke or some other medical emergency. I went outside, believing I needed to be somewhere public in case I lost consciousness. Once I got outside and started feeling better, it dawned on me that I'd had a panic attack, fueled by my perception of "DANGER" translating into a weird sensation of unreality.

Other common beliefs in panic disorder include:

- If I panic while driving, I'll crash the car.
- If my panic attack gets bad enough, I'll faint.
- Everyone will know I'm panicking, and I'll embarrass myself.
- If I panic I might lose control and attack someone.
- Panic will make me lose my vision, which could be really dangerous.
- If I don't stop panicking, I'm going to go crazy.
- I'm having a heart attack.
- I might not get enough air and suffocate from a panic attack.
- I'm going to have sudden diarrhea if I panic at the wrong time.

If you struggle with panic, think about specific times you've had a panic attack. What triggered the attack? Did you interpret the trigger in a way that led to more fear and more panic?

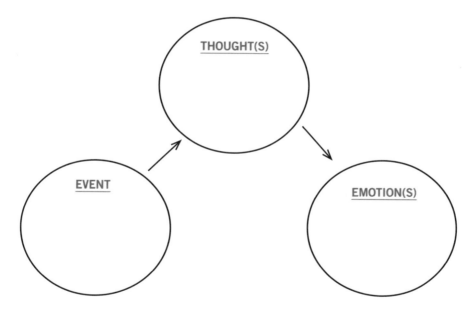

SOCIAL ANXIETY DISORDER

The driving thought in social anxiety disorder is that you'll do something to embarrass yourself around other people. If we're prone to social anxiety, we're likely to make the most negative possible interpretation of things that happen in social settings. One big challenge in social anxiety disorder is that we're often afraid that others will know we're anxious. "They'll see I'm blushing and think I'm an idiot for being embarrassed," we might tell ourselves. Or we might think, "If my voice shakes, they'll lose all confidence in me." The anxiety about appearing anxious tends to heighten our anxiety, leading to a vicious cycle.

If you experience a lot of social anxiety, think about a recent situation in which you feared others' judgments. Can you identify thoughts about what might happen in this situation?

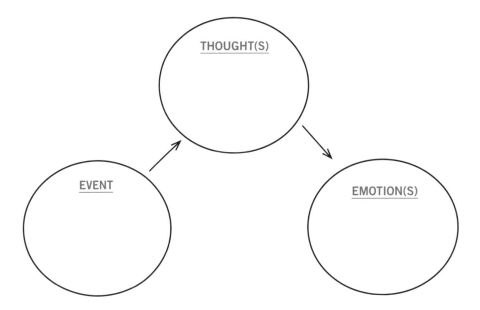

GENERALIZED ANXIETY DISORDER (GAD)

Thinking tends to be a very prominent part of GAD. The thoughts often start with **"What if . . . ?"** about something bad that could happen:

- What if I fail this exam?
- What if my headache means I have a brain tumor?
- What if something happens to my parents?
- What if I lose my job?
- What if the stock market tanks and wipes out my retirement savings?

Because it's "generalized," the worry in GAD can attach to anything. There also tends to be an implicit belief that *I need to do something to make sure this bad thing doesn't happen*. We feel like it's our responsibility to control the situation, whatever it may be. We might tell ourselves we have to *"make sure that doesn't happen,"* and so we'll do some mental activity (worrying) to try to work through the problem, but unproductively. It's like trying to play an entire chess game in advance, not knowing the other player's moves, but still trying to "solve" the upcoming game.

Unfortunately, the things we worry about typically aren't completely under our control. Can we be absolutely certain we won't fail an exam, have a medical crisis, lose someone close to us, and so forth? So we find ourselves caught in a thinking loop: From *What if*, we try to think of a solution that *makes sure* what we're afraid of doesn't happen. Since we can't have the certainty we seek, we're back to *What if . . . .*

For example, we might worry about our kids' safety: *What if they get badly hurt at camp?* We run through a list of bad things that might happen and try to reassure ourselves that our children will be fine. But of course we can't *know* they'll really be safe, so our minds go back to *What if*, and the loop continues.

A person with GAD may also believe that worrying is a useful exercise. We might think, for example, that if we worry about something, we can prevent it from happening, and so to stop worrying would be to let down our guard. It's easy to believe our worrying "works" if we're always worrying and what we've worried about hasn't happened—maybe it's because we worried! Or we might believe that our constant worrying says something good about us—*that we care.*

If you see yourself as someone who worries too much, think about a recent situation that triggered anxiety. What was the situation, and can you identify any thoughts that led to your distress?

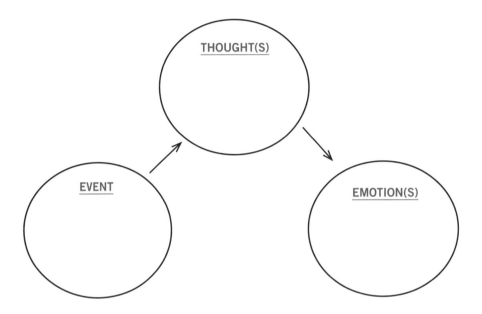

FEAR OF FEAR

It's not hard to understand thoughts about situations or objects we believe are dangerous—our fear is tied to our belief about the danger. But what about situations or objects we *know* aren't really dangerous but we still avoid and are afraid of?

Often we are afraid of our own fear. We may think it's dangerous to be extremely afraid, and that something catastrophic might happen if we become too frightened. Maybe we think we'll have a heart attack or a stroke. We might also believe that our fear will last forever if we confront what we're afraid of.

Not uncommonly we fear we'll "lose it" or "go crazy" from being too afraid. We may believe on some level that if we get too terrified, we can reach a place that's "beyond fear," some qualitatively different experience that's worse than bad. Maybe we think we'll get so "freaked out" that we "won't be able to stand it" and will do something embarrassing.

Think about your own experiences of fear and anxiety. Are there things you're afraid of even though you know they aren't dangerous? Think as carefully as you can about how you feel when confronted with the object or situation. Do you have any predictions about what will happen as a result of being terrified? Write your thoughts in the space below.

COMMON THEMES IN DEPRESSION

Neil got a second interview at a company that seemed like a good fit for him. Then a curious thing started to happen: He began to assume that there must be something wrong with the company, because why else would they want to hire him? He felt ashamed when he told his wife about the interview—he wasn't even going to tell her about it, but she asked where his interview was when she saw he'd set out his suit.

Neil and I worked together to understand his thought process. He discovered he was telling himself the company must be really desperate to hire someone if they were still interested in him after knowing his age. As a result he told himself he was pathetic for interviewing with the company.

When we're depressed, we often see any disappointing event as evidence of our own failure. Sometimes we even turn positive events into negative ones. Depressed thinking can turn even a win into a loss. Common thoughts in depression center around themes of being "less than" in some way. Examples include:

- I'm weak.
- I'm a loser.
- No one could really love someone like me.
- I mess up everything.

Hopelessness is another common theme in depressed thinking, and it leads to an attitude of "Why bother?" *If nothing we do makes things better*, we reason, *why waste our energy trying to change things*? This kind of thinking can feed itself, since it leads to inactivity, continued low mood, and an ongoing belief that things will never improve.

If you're going through depression, think of a recent time something really brought down your mood. What did you tell yourself about what happened? Maybe even while reading this chapter you've had depression-fueled thoughts, such as "This probably won't work for me," or "What's the point? I *know* my thoughts don't make sense. Nothing can help me." Take some time to record what happened and what thoughts you can recall.

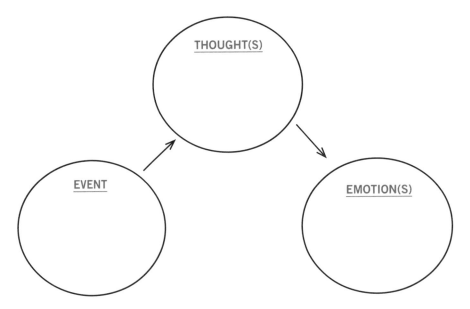

Getting to the Core

Over time, Neil noticed that all of his thoughts shared a "final destination." If he traced where all the thoughts led, he discovered that they all ended with his being useless and pathetic. He even had an image in mind that went along with this notion—he pictured a worn-out washcloth that's been dropped between the washer and dryer, and nobody bothers to pick it up. We diagrammed his thoughts like this:

Neil's Core Belief Diagram

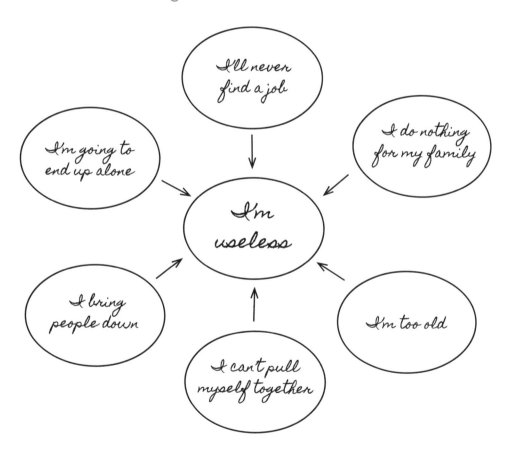

The central thought or image reflects what Aaron Beck and others call a "core belief," with the specific thoughts all coming from and strengthening this central belief:

- Believing that I'm generally useless and pathetic leads to more specific thoughts that are related to my core belief.
- Those specific thoughts are taken as "evidence" supporting my core belief. Without identifying and checking these thoughts, the cycle continues.

We find a similar phenomenon with anxiety, which is our "core fear," or the "big fear" that drives our smaller fears. If I have a core fear of dying and abandoning my kids, for example, I may be extremely anxious about getting sick, traveling, and safety in the home.

You may have an inkling, at this point, about what your core beliefs and fears are. Or maybe you have no idea yet. Over the coming days and weeks, you'll be gathering information that will help you identify your core beliefs and fears. Once we've pinpointed these central issues, we can work more efficiently, recognizing that it's basically the same message our mind keeps sending us.

Practice for This Week

In the coming week, pay attention to times when you notice a worsening in your mood. As close in time to the event as possible—ideally in "real time"—see if you can catch the thoughts that are feeding your emotions. Keep the Identifying Thoughts forms on hand so you can complete them as soon as possible. Next week, we'll use what you come up with to begin breaking away from these thought patterns.

In this chapter, you took another important step: you began to figure out some of your thoughts that lead you to anxiety and depression. I encourage you to treat any progress you make this week as a success. Most of us have to work hard to discover our underlying thoughts, so if you find it isn't easy, you're in good company. Stick with it. You are also continuing the work you started last week of adding valued activities into your schedule.

Take some time to think about how you're feeling at this point. Write your thoughts and feelings, along with any questions, in the space below. I'll see you in week 4.

_____

_____

_____

_____

_____

_____

_____

_____

_____

_____

_____

_____

_____

_____

_____

ACTIVITY PLAN

1 Complete the four activities you planned for this week.
2 Complete the Identifying Thoughts form for at least three events.
3 Plan a time now to return to complete week 4.

Breaking Negative Thought Patterns

Welcome back. In week 3, we continued planning activities to add into your life. You had four activities planned for the past week; in the space below, summarize what went well with the activities.

_____

_____

_____

_____

_____

_____

_____

_____

_____

_____

_____

Was anything different than you expected—any challenges you ran into, or pleasant surprises?

_____

_____

_____

_____

_____

_____

_____

_____

What did you learn from these activities that you can apply in upcoming weeks?

_____

_____

_____

_____

_____

_____

Based on your experiences last week, choose _five_ activities from your list and follow the same procedure as in past weeks, scheduling days and times to complete the activities. Choose from your more challenging activities (2s and 3s) if they seem doable.

If there were activities from last week that you did not complete, do you still believe they are worth doing? If so, consider ways to raise the odds of completing them, such as breaking them down into still smaller tasks. (See page 80, "Raising the Odds," to review as needed.) Write your five activities on the next page:

Activity 1:

_____

Activity 2:

_____

Activity 3:

_____

Activity 4:

_____

Activity 5:

_____

Now, find places in your calendar to schedule these activities for the coming week.

In week 3, you also began monitoring your thought patterns. You were to complete the Identifying Thoughts form for at least three events. Review the records you kept over the past week. Do any themes stand out?

_____

_____

_____

_____

_____

_____

_____

Alex Breaks Through

"It was confirmation of everything I've thought was wrong with me," Alex said as her voice broke. "I'm letting everyone down. They're depending on me, and I can't even get myself together." She wiped away tears and sat with her hand over her eyes.

Earlier in the week, Alex's supervisor Dianne had called Alex into her office. Dianne told her she needed to be putting in more hours, including evening and weekends, if she wanted to meet the expectations of her job. She reminded Alex that she herself did what she had to do 20 years earlier, as a mother with young kids, and that women have to prove their dedication to their work to be taken seriously. Alex left the meeting promising to make more of an effort, and feeling completely demoralized.

Four weeks earlier, Alex had started treatment with me. She was struggling to find time for a demanding job as assistant director of a large executive MBA program and raising two young daughters. Her life was all work and no play: Her day started with the frantic morning routine from 5:30 to 7:30 a.m., then shuttling her four-year-old to preschool and her 18-month-old to day care, then on to a grueling day at the office till 6:00.

Her mother would watch the kids in the late afternoon till she got home. Then, the nighttime crunch happened till both kids were down around 7:30 p.m. Alex and her husband, Simon, might have 15 minutes to talk about their day while cleaning the kitchen before they each did their nightly chores and prepared for the next day. She often brought home files to review at night and was always amazed by how little she managed to do before it was 10:30 p.m. and she was falling asleep sitting up.

Since her younger daughter was born, Alex hadn't been sleeping well. Her nerves were frayed and she was often irritable, which was never her personality before. She wished she were more patient with her kids. "This morning I heard my four-year-old tell her sister to stop fussing because 'Mommy's cranky this morning,'" she told me. "I felt like such a failure as a mother."

In the first couple of weeks of her treatment, we focused on finding small ways for Alex to fit a few enjoyable and restorative activities into her days. For example, she asked Simon to watch the girls on Saturday mornings so she could go to a spin class with a friend. She also realized that listening to classical music on her drive home from work was more relaxing than being bombarded by bad news on the radio—and it didn't take up any more of her precious time. She had just started monitoring her thoughts during difficult events for the past week, including the encounter with her supervisor.

This week it's time to examine your thoughts. By paying attention to what your mind is telling you, you may have started to notice some problems with your thoughts. For example, you may have realized that not all your thoughts were 100 percent true. You might have noticed your thoughts gravitated toward certain negative interpretations, even when other ones were possible. If you noticed any such tendencies, record them below. If you didn't, don't worry—you'll have plenty of opportunities to examine your thinking.

_____

_____

_____

_____

_____

_____

_____

_____

_____

_____

As we covered in chapter 1, our thoughts can have powerful effects on our emotions. When we're depressed or anxious, our thoughts can fall into patterns that aren't helpful to us.

Unhelpful Thoughts

Consider all the ways thinking is helpful to us. We can plan for the future, consider our past actions, evaluate others' motives, savor our favorite memories, and so forth. When our thoughts are a good enough fit with reality, they serve us well.

Some of the thoughts you recorded over the past week may be accurate, and therefore helpful. Our minds can also create thoughts that *do not accurately reflect reality*:

- We make predictions that are wrong.
- We misunderstand someone's intent.
- We misread a situation.

We all make errors in our thinking. After a talk I once gave as part of a job interview, I was certain my audience had been bored and severely underwhelmed. "I blew it," I thought as I walked home. When I got home, there was an e-mail in my inbox offering me the job. Fortunately *we can think about our own thinking* and recognize when our thoughts do and don't make sense.

Think of a time when you thought or believed something that turned out to be verifiably false, and describe it in the space below.

_____

_____

_____

_____

_____

_____

_____

_____

_____

_____

LABELING ERRORS IN THINKING

Thinking errors have been described in various ways:

- **Irrational:** Albert Ellis emphasized that our thoughts often **don't make sense**. For example, we might tell ourselves that everyone must think well of us or we'll be terribly upset. Ellis's rational emotive behavior therapy was designed to identify irrational thinking and replace it with rational thoughts that would lead to greater well-being.

- **Dysfunctional:** In Aaron Beck's cognitive therapy, errors in thinking are called "dysfunctional" because they **don't serve us well**. When we tell ourselves "There's no use in trying, anyway," for example, we're setting ourselves up to fail. By identifying dysfunctional thought patterns, we can work to replace them with thoughts that help us move toward our goals.

- **Biased:** A large number of studies have shown how **one-sided** our thoughts tend to be when we're anxious and depressed. For example, in social anxiety disorder a person is likely to notice potentially negative feedback from others and to ignore positive feedback. By paying attention only to information that supports our anxiety and depression, we strengthen our negative thought patterns.

- **Distorted:** Finally, errors in thinking **don't accurately reflect reality**. We might think we're completely incompetent after making a minor error, or that *nobody* likes us because one person treated us unkindly. Through cognitive therapy we can change our thinking to better match reality.

These ways of describing thinking errors are related; for example, biased thoughts are likely to be distorted, and irrational thoughts will almost certainly be dysfunctional. You might keep these different labels in mind as you identify and challenge your own thought patterns.

EXAMINING THE EVIDENCE

One of the episodes Alex recorded involved a particularly stressful morning trying to get everyone out the door on time. She felt irritated and overwhelmed and thought gloomily on her drive to work, "I am such a disappointment."

As we talked about this thought, it was clear she meant it in a global way: "I am nothing but a big disappointment to everyone." She found this belief very upsetting. We needed to think carefully together about this thought. Was it true?

We first looked for evidence to support Alex's thought, and there were indeed times that others were disappointed in her, like her supervisor recently and her kids when she snapped at them.

We then considered evidence against her thought. Could she think of anything that contradicted it? She thought for a moment and said, "My older daughter does tell me sometimes that I'm a good Mommy, 'even though you yell sometimes.'" She added this fact to the "Evidence Against . . ." column. We continued this exercise, and then looked at the columns side by side:

Evidence for my thought	Evidence against my thought
• Dianne was disappointed in me.	• Dianne also said I'm doing good work.
• I'm often irritable toward my girls.	• Libby sometimes tells me I'm a good Mom.
	• My husband says I'm handling a lot.
	• I'm working full-time and raising two daughters.

I asked Alex what she thinks of the original thought now.

"It's a little one-sided," she admitted.

"What does it leave out?" I asked her.

"Well, the times that I don't disappoint people."

We worked to revise her thought to better fit the data she had collected. She wrote, "Lately I've been disappointing people more often than I want to."

I asked her which of the two thoughts was a better reflection of reality. She decided her revised thought made more sense, even though her original thought "felt" right in some way. I asked her what she felt when she read each thought. The first one, she said, felt like a crushing weight. The second one felt sad, but like "a sadness I can handle."

She said to me, "Maybe I'm more than a disappointment." Her eyes filled with tears, and several moments passed before she could speak. Finally she said, "For so long I've assumed I was failing miserably, and now it feels like almost too much to hope for that there might still be hope for me."

Notice in this example that the goal was not for Alex to "think happy thoughts" to neutralize negative ones. The goal was to take a hard, clear-eyed look at her situation—and her thinking about it—and to make an accurate judgment. If she actually was a disappointment in every way, that information would be important for us to have.

Let's work through your own recorded thoughts. First, choose the event you found most upsetting. Using the form on the following page, record the evidence that supports your thought. Is there any evidence against your thought, suggesting it might not tell the whole story?

Event:	Thought:	Emotion:
_____	_____	_____
_____	_____	_____
_____	_____	_____
_____	_____	_____

Evidence for my thought	Evidence against my thought
_____	_____
_____	_____
_____	_____
_____	_____
_____	_____
_____	_____
_____	_____

You can find a copy of this form online at callistomediabooks.com/cbt.

Based on the evidence that you reviewed, how accurate is the thought you had?

_____

_____

How would you modify the thought to make it fit better with reality?

_____

_____

_____

_____

SEEING THE POSITIVE

Alex had just told me about a time she was feeling horrible about herself. She and Simon had decided he would take the girls to a birthday party for one of Libby's classmates so Alex could get together with a friend. She felt guilty about not going to the party and started recalling every other time she'd missed kids' events.

We began to examine her thought, "I do nothing for my kids." I asked her to describe where she was when she had this thought and what was happening.

She said, "I had told Libby that Simon would be taking her to the party, and I couldn't tell if she was okay with it or not. Later in the evening, I was lying in Libby's bed scratching her arm like she likes me to do to help her fall asleep. I kept adding to a mental list of ways I'd let down my kids."

I asked her, "Where did you say you were when you had this thought?"

She started to tell me again, and then stopped herself. "Oh—I get it. That was a therapist question." She gave a half-smile. "I suppose that's ironic, my thinking I do nothing while I'm in the middle of trying to take care of Libby?"

We talked for a while about the mind's ability to see what it wants to and ignore the rest, even when it's right in front of us.

As we search for evidence for and against our thoughts, we need to be as open as possible to all available information. If our thoughts are biased in a negative direction, we are already overlooking some relevant information. If we're not careful, we can allow this bias to dominate our efforts to break negative thought patterns, which defeats the purpose.

Return to the example you were working on before. As you test the accuracy of your thinking, take care to consider whether you might be ignoring information that would support more positive thoughts.

Challenging our thoughts is not about lying to ourselves and denying our imperfections. We're smart enough to see through it if we try to trick ourselves.

A big part of this practice is to grow toward *accepting* our imperfections, and not hating ourselves for being fully human.

Let's take a look at our tendency at times to see things as worse than they are.

IS IT A CATASTROPHE?

So far we've focused on thinking errors that involve bias or false predictions. We might think that getting a parking ticket means we're horribly irresponsible, or that we'll faint if we panic, or that people won't want to be friends with us if we show signs of anxiety. Each of these thinking errors involves mistaken beliefs.

But what about thoughts that aren't unrealistic? For example, what if our fear is that we'll blush when we speak up in a meeting, or that we'll have a panic attack on a plane? There might be a reasonably high chance that these things will happen. Often, in these cases, our error lies in *how bad we think the outcome is or would be*. We might believe that if we blush it will be *awful*, or that having a panic attack on a plane will be a *total disaster*. Our minds can treat an awkward, uncomfortable, or disappointing situation as if it's a complete catastrophe.

As you examine your own thoughts, do you notice any emotional reactions that seem overblown based on the thought you identified? For example, did you tell yourself that something you did was "awful," or that it would be "unbearable" if your fear came true? If that's the case, consider whether you might have told your-self something more—something that could be driving your emotional responses. Record your observations in the space below.

_____

_____

_____

_____

_____

_____

_____

WHAT WOULD YOU TELL SOMEONE YOU LOVE?

As we continued to examine Alex's upsetting thoughts, she described an episode in which her four-year-old refused to get dressed in the morning. "I'd had a terrible night's sleep, and I had to be at work on time for a meeting with all the new MBA students. Libby said she couldn't get dressed because Bunny, her favorite stuffed animal, was sleeping in her room and she didn't want to wake her up. I got so frustrated with her that finally I got down on her eye level and said, 'Put your dress on now or Bunny goes in the trash.' Even as I said it I thought to myself, 'You're a terrible mother. Who does that to her kid?'"

I asked Alex what she would say to someone she loved if he or she told her they'd done something similar.

She smiled and said, "It's funny; that actually came up over the weekend. I was running with Laura, and I told her how upset I was at myself for losing patience and threatening to get rid of Bunny. 'That's nothing,' she told me. 'You'd be shocked to hear some of the things that come out of my mouth when the kids are really aggravating me.' She told me some of them, and to be honest—I was kind of shocked. I mean, it wasn't anything abusive, but I would feel terrible if I said those things."

"So that must have really changed your feelings about Laura, huh?" I asked her.

"How do you mean?" Alex replied.

"Well, based on how you felt toward yourself for doing something more mild, Laura must be a terrible mother."

Alex frowned. "No, she's actually a great mom. She loves her kids. She just juggles a lot, raising kids and working full time, and sometimes they get on her nerves and she says things she regrets."

"You'll have to pardon the comparison, but it sounds a lot like you were describing yourself."

"I know what you're getting at," Alex said, "and I can see how everything I said could apply to me. It just ... feels different. I mean, I could never say to her the things I say to myself. I love Laura."

I asked her, "What would you say to Alex if you loved her?"

Alex thought about this question during the week. When she came back, she said she'd been practicing talking to herself "like I'm someone I care about." She said at times she even felt a sense of caring for herself, and also of being cared for. "It feels weird to say this," she said, "but I'm starting to think it's not my job to run myself into the ground."

I asked her what kinds of thoughts she'd been working on, especially in situations that would trigger her self-loathing thoughts.

"I tell myself, 'You made a mistake, and that's okay.' The other day I lost patience with my kids on the drive to school, and I heard that familiar critical voice saying, 'Why couldn't you have held on for just a few minutes longer? Now you've ruined everyone's day.'

"And I answered the voice. I said, 'Because this morning, as much as I wanted to, I just couldn't. And maybe the day's not ruined—not yet.' I actually smiled. I know I'm not a perfect mother ... and I can live with that. I'm also not a disaster."

Most of the time, the thinking errors we make apply only to ourselves. For reasons that aren't entirely clear, we're almost always harder on ourselves than we are on others. We rarely would make the same interpretation if the same event happened to someone else.

For many of us, practicing a gentler way of talking to ourselves will feel strange at first. We may have gotten so accustomed to being harsh with ourselves that we believe we deserve to be talked to that way. With practice, a kinder approach can start to feel more natural.

Now, choose another event that you recorded over the past week and use the Challenging Your Thoughts form below to examine your thought or thoughts.

Event:	Thought:	Emotion:
_____	_____	_____
_____	_____	_____
_____	_____	_____
_____	_____	_____
_____	_____	_____
_____	_____	_____

Evidence for my thought	Evidence against my thought
_____	_____
_____	_____
_____	_____
_____	_____
_____	_____
_____	_____
_____	_____
_____	_____

You can find a copy of this form online at callistomediabooks.com/cbt.

Remember to consider the following points in your examination of the evidence:

1 Am I ignoring any evidence that would contradict my thoughts?
2 How likely is it that I'm seeing it as worse than it really is?
3 What would I say to someone I care about if they had this thought?

Based on your examination of the evidence, would you revise your thought in any way to better fit the evidence you came up with? If so, write it below.

A more reality-based thought is:

_____

_____

Common Thinking Errors in Anxiety and Depression

By now, you may have begun to recognize recurrent errors in your thinking. While everyone's thoughts are somewhat unique, in the previous chapter we considered predictable themes that show up in depression and anxiety. Let's revisit these themes as we consider the common thinking errors in each condition.

DEPRESSION

As we saw with Alex, depression is linked to thoughts about ourselves that are overly negative, as Aaron Beck and colleagues described in their manual on cognitive therapy for depression. We might assume we'll fail, or that if we failed it's because we're defective in some fundamental way. When things go wrong, we'll take it personally and may assume we'll *always* mess things up.

If you deal with depression, look for signs that your thoughts about yourself are harsher than they need to be, based on the facts. When we take a close look at our depression-related thoughts and assumptions, we often find they're unfounded, or at best loosely based in reality. Also look for thoughts that start with "I should." These kinds of thoughts are often heavy-handed and not based in reality.

Alex found herself making "should" statements that were in direct conflict. First she told herself, "I should be spending more time at work" after Dianne confronted her. Later in the week, she found herself saying, "I should be spending more time with my girls." She realized that without invoking magic, there was no way she could live up to one of these demands without sacrificing the other.

As a more realistic alternative, Alex's revised thought was: "This is a busy and demanding time in my life. I wish I had time to do everything perfectly, but that's not the way the world works."

Remember: The goal in questioning our negative thoughts is not to convince ourselves that nothing is our fault. Rather, we want to see ourselves more clearly, faults and all. We can practice seeing our imperfections as part of the whole picture of who we are. In the process, maybe we can take ourselves a little less seriously and begin to value ourselves as full human beings.

If you've been depressed, summarize below any errors you've become aware of in your own thinking. What led you to recognize them as errors?

Example: I assume people don't like me once they get to know me, even though a lot of evidence suggests my friends like me—like the fact that two people texted me this week about getting together.

ANXIETY

When we're highly anxious, we tend to overestimate the probability that what we're afraid of will happen. In panic disorder, for example, we often believe (erroneously) that panic leads to fainting or suffocation. We might also believe that panicking makes us likely to do something dangerous like impulsively jump from a bridge, when our instinct is to actually move *away from* danger when we panic. If we're afraid of flying in an airplane, we might be surprised how small the actual risk is.

Consider the things that cause you a lot of anxiety. Did you identify any errors in your beliefs related to the things you're afraid of?

Example: When I have a physical symptom, I often assume it's the worst possible disease rather than something more benign (which so far it's always been).

_____

_____

_____

_____

_____

_____

_____

_____

_____

_____

We can also exaggerate the *cost* of the outcome we're afraid of. In social anxiety, for example, we often believe it's awful to show embarrassment (like by blushing), but there's evidence that people actually think kindly of someone who blushes. We also might cringe over and over as we remember something foolish we said, and imagine that others are still thinking about it. In reality, chances are they've moved on to other things, just like we do when someone else makes a social misstep.

Have you noticed that some of the things you're afraid of happening might be more manageable than you thought? Write your thoughts in the space below.

_____

_____

_____

_____

_____

_____

Finally, we might discover we have beliefs about our anxiety that don't hold up to inspection. As discussed in the previous chapter, we are often afraid of our own fear, believing we "can't handle it" if we get too scared, or that being very afraid is dangerous. We often think we'll be overwhelmed if we face our fears, and that somehow they'll destroy us.

If the thing we fear is not truly dangerous, then in fact there is minimal risk from facing it. Fear _per se_ is unpleasant and uncomfortable, but not dangerous. This fact is essential to keep in mind when we get to week 6 with its focus on facing our fears. Knowing that fear isn't dangerous can motivate us to face what we're afraid of.

Did you discover errors in the way you think about your own fear? What led you to think that the thoughts are not correct?

_____

_____

_____

_____

_____

_____

_____

Identifying Your Core Beliefs and Fears

Last week, we looked at the ideas of a core belief and a core fear. Alex recorded several episodes of her upsetting thoughts, and she identified the following core belief:

Alex's Core Belief Diagram

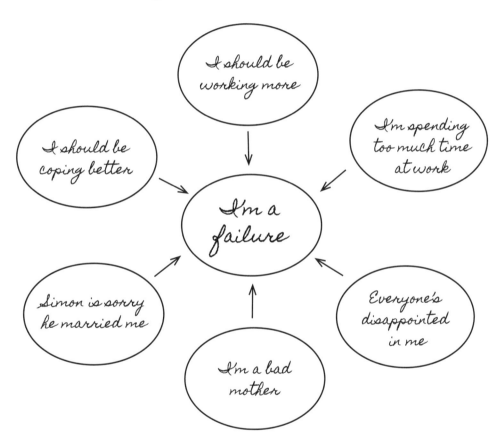

As Alex began to recognize a familiar refrain in her thinking, it got easier for her to see what her mind was up to and to dismiss the thoughts about being a failure. After a while, she rarely needed to make a formal record of her thinking—she could adjust her thoughts to more realistic ones "on the fly." She even developed a shorthand response to her negative thoughts: "Someone's lying about me again," she would say to herself, as a reminder not to believe the thought. At times, she would replace the thoughts, while other times she would simply disregard the misguided thought and move on.

Each of us can identify our core beliefs and fears. Based on what you've observed of your thoughts so far, what are common themes and errors that emerge in your thought records?

_____

_____

_____

_____

_____

_____

_____

_____

_____

_____

_____

_____

_____

_____

_____

_____

Using these observations, complete the diagram below as best you can to indicate your core belief/fear and related thoughts.

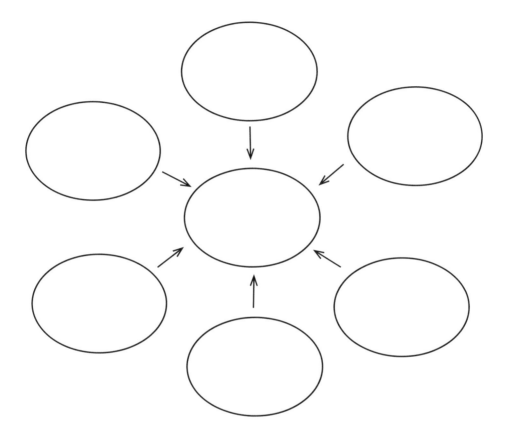

You can find a copy of this form online at callistomediabooks.com/cbt.

Over time, we can develop streamlined ways to respond to our thoughts as we get more adept at dismissing them and seeing more accurate alternatives. For now, I encourage you to continue completing the forms for challenging your thoughts. Structured practice is a good investment in learning the skill well. This week, choose three triggering events and complete the Challenging Your Thoughts form for each one.

In this chapter, we built on the work you did last week and began actively challenging any misguided thoughts that drive your emotions. You're also continuing the activity scheduling that you started two weeks ago.

You're now more than halfway through this seven-week program. Excellent work making it this far. Hopefully, by now, you're beginning to see some benefit from the time and energy you've invested.

In the remaining weeks, we'll continue working on the things you've done so far. Next week we'll also begin to address effective ways of managing time and getting things done.

Take a few moments to reflect on how things are going so far. What seems to be going well? Where do you still find yourself struggling? Of the things you've worked on so far, which ones feel like they may be the most important for you? Write your thoughts and feelings in the space below.

_____

_____

_____

_____

_____

_____

_____

_____

_____

_____

_____

_____

ACTIVITY PLAN

1 Complete your five scheduled activities.
2 Complete a Challenging Your Thoughts form for three situations this week.
3 Plan a time now to complete week 5.

Time and Task Management

Last week, you continued planning enjoyable and important activities, and you began actively confronting your unhelpful thoughts. This week, we'll continue with these techniques. We'll also turn to the topic of managing our time well and completing tasks effectively.

Review the list of five activities you planned to complete (page 106). How did they go? Record anything that stands out in the space below.

_____

_____

_____

_____

_____

Choose five more activities from your list to complete in the coming week. Carefully consider which ones to do, and don't be afraid to challenge yourself with some of your hardest activities. There's a good chance the more difficult activities are the more rewarding ones.

Activity 1:

_____

Activity 2:

_____

Activity 3:

_____

Activity 4:

_____

Activity 5:

_____

As always, plan in your calendar specific times to do your activities.

Lastly, review the Challenging Your Thoughts forms you completed (pages 113 and 118). In the space below, summarize the kinds of thinking errors (if any) you noticed. Did they cluster around a core theme?

_____

_____

_____

_____

_____

_____

_____

We'll continue to work on addressing your thinking patterns. If you struggled with challenging your thoughts, consider reviewing week 4. In the coming week, complete at least one Challenging Your Thoughts form, and more if necessary.

Time Management with Walter

It was Walter's spring break from college, and instead of spending it at the beach with his friends, he was in my office. In the fall semester, he was struggling with depression, and he had to take two Incompletes. As much as he'd wanted to, he hadn't managed to finish the coursework over the winter break, and now he was falling behind in his classes again.

"I wanted so badly to do well," Walter told me. "My parents were thrilled when I got into this school, and I did all right freshman year. But some things happened over the summer before my sophomore year that made it feel like I was already in a hole when school started in September."

One of Walter's friends had died suddenly and unexpectedly in July. The death was a shock to Walter, causing him to focus on the sad and scary aspects of life. There was also stress in his family, because his parents had run into financial difficulties. While nobody talked about it, he also sensed that his mother had developed a drinking problem. Taken together, the summer was a confusing and alienating time for Walter, and he returned to school feeling anxious and alone.

Walter found it hard to complete his work. As soon as he sat down in the library and took out his class notes, a wave of dread would wash over him. He described trying to review lecture slides, and inevitably he would end up on social media, scanning through his friends' posts. By the time the library was closing, he'd have accomplished nothing besides feeling bad that his life wasn't as exciting as his friends'. He would walk back to his dorm room feeling frustrated and overwhelmed, promising himself he'd do his work before going to bed.

In his room, he'd be seized by fear about not understanding the course material and failing, and would spend most of his time surfing the Web or binge watching various programs until he was too tired to stay awake. "I'll get up early and do it then," he'd tell himself. Usually he ended up sleeping late and missing his morning classes.

By the end of the semester, it was clear he couldn't finish everything, and he managed to scrape through with a B- and a C+ in his easier classes. He got permission from his other two instructors to take Incompletes for the semester, with the understanding that he would complete the work over the winter break. However, he continued his pattern of avoidance, and the longer he delayed doing the work the harder it was to make himself do it.

When he returned to campus in the spring, Walter vowed to do things differently. But as the first round of midterm exams approached, he found himself slipping into old patterns of behavior. By the time spring break came, he was in another academic crisis, and he didn't know how to stop his downward slide.

Effects of Depression and Anxiety on Time and Task Management

As it is with so many of us, Walter's depression and anxiety made it hard for him to take care of things. When we're depressed, it's hard to find motivation. High levels of anxiety don't help, either, since they can lead to avoiding the very things we need to do. Both anxiety and depression can make it hard to concentrate and interfere with our ability to be effective problem solvers. As we struggle to fulfill our commitments, our depression and anxiety can worsen, perpetuating a familiar cycle.

How have depression and/or anxiety affected your ability to complete tasks?

_____

_____

_____

_____

_____

_____

_____

_____

Fortunately, the work you've done so far has already introduced some relevant skills—skills this chapter will build on. For example, we looked at ways to increase your odds of completing an activity when we discussed behavioral activation (pages 70-71). The thinking skills you've been working on will also be helpful as we look at some of the thoughts that can interfere with effectively using our time.

Take a few moments to think about your own time management. What do you tend to do well in managing your time? What strategies work well for you?

_____

_____

_____

_____

_____

_____

_____

_____

Are there also areas where you struggle with managing your time? Do you feel constantly rushed, or like everything you do takes too long? Is it hard to decide how best to spend your time? Do you find yourself putting things off as long as possible? Write your reflections in the space below.

_____

_____

_____

_____

_____

_____

_____

_____

In the upcoming sections, we'll build on the things you're already doing well to address the challenges you may be having with time management.

Principles of Time and Task Management

Perhaps more than any other topic in this book, the principles of managing our time well can be patently obvious. Regardless, the most important point is that you systematically apply these principles to your life.

The system we'll use is based on the strategy of breaking big tasks into manageable parts. Most of the time, what's hard about getting things done is that the project seems too big. Trying to do a challenging task is like running a long race: We can't do it all at once, but we can do it a step at a time.

The basic approach is to:

1 **Identify your tasks:** Decide what you need to do.
2 **Prioritize your tasks:** Determine where to start, based on when things are due.
3 **Plan when to complete your tasks:** Assign a time on your calendar for each task.
4 **Follow through on completing tasks:** No step is more important than actually doing what you set out to do.

USING CBT TO ADDRESS DIFFICULTY SLEEPING

When we sleep poorly, it's harder to manage our time well and get things done. Poor time management can also interfere with sleep. It's a good idea to devote some attention to getting better sleep if yours has suffered.

The most effective treatment for bad sleep is CBT for insomnia, or CBT-I. Four to eight sessions can make a huge difference in a person's sleep. The main principles of treatment are:

- **Stick to a consistent bedtime and wakeup time.** By staying on a regular schedule, your body knows when it's time to sleep and when it's time to be awake, and it's easier to fall asleep and sleep soundly.

- **Don't spend more time in bed than you're able to sleep.** If you're able to sleep seven hours per night on average but you spend nine hours in bed, you'll have two hours that you're awake in bed (and probably stressed about not sleeping) or sleeping poorly. By spending less time in bed, we actually wind up getting more sleep. The average participant in CBT-I gets an additional 43 minutes of sleep while spending 47 *fewer* minutes in bed—which is time we can invest in other activities.

- **Get out of bed if you're not able to fall asleep.** If you know sleep isn't coming anytime soon, do something else in another room (like reading or watching a favorite show). Return to bed when you feel sleepy. Repeat as necessary. It's better to spend time doing something you enjoy than lying in bed feeling frustrated. This guideline applies at any point in the "sleep window"—beginning, middle, or end.

- **Generally avoid napping.** When we nap during the day, we decrease our body's drive for sleep, which can make it hard to fall asleep and sleep soundly at night. If you do nap, plan to do it earlier in the day and keep it short.

- **Avoid caffeine later in the day.** As a rule of thumb, caffeine after lunchtime is likely to interfere with nighttime sleep. Depending on your sensitivity to its effects, you may need to avoid caffeine even earlier.

- **Remember that a bad night's sleep is almost certainly not a disaster.** It's easy for us to panic when we can't sleep and to think we'll "be a wreck" the next day. In reality, we usually can function adequately, even if at times we're sleepier than normal.

If you continue to struggle with poor sleep, consider making an appointment with a sleep specialist.

Take a moment to consider this approach. Do you notice any steps that seem to give you particular trouble? For example, do you struggle to prioritize tasks because everything seems important and you don't know where to begin? Do you make a good plan for getting things done and then struggle to complete it?

_____

_____

_____

_____

_____

_____

MAKING THE MOST OF YOUR TIME

Each of us is given a finite amount of time, in our lives and in each day. The time we have gives us countless opportunities, which also introduces a problem: How do we make the best use of finite time, given infinite possibilities?

Each of us is trustee of the time we're allotted on Earth, so we might consider time management sacred work. While *time* management and *task* management are two sides of the same coin, the time we have is non-negotiable since obviously we can't create more of it. Tasks, on the other hand, are more flexible, because we can do them now, later, or not at all.

It can be freeing to shift your focus to how you're spending your time and away from what you're accomplishing. We can ask ourselves each day, "How can I spend this day well?" As long as we've spent our time doing our most important tasks and being engaged in the experience, what we don't accomplish is largely irrelevant.

If you find yourself saying things like, "I don't have enough time," consider whether it's possible to shift toward a focus on simply using your time as well as possible. The time we have is the time we have. If we can make friends with the time we're given, we can focus our efforts on making the best use of it.

For the following sections you'll need your calendar, so make sure you have it on hand. It can be an electronic calendar or a hard copy—whichever works for you. Just make sure it has all your appointments in it, rather than having separate calendars for different parts of your life (for example, separate work and home calendars).

IDENTIFYING TASKS

"What do you need to do?" I asked Walter.

He shook his head. "So much," he said. "It feels impossible."

"Let's find out if it is," I said. Together we made a list of all of Walter's outstanding assignments, including the Incompletes from last fall. His list looked like this:

- Finish Incompletes
- Read six chapters of psych textbook
- Six math problem sets
- Two experiments for intro psych
- Write History paper

As we looked at his list together, Walter said he had mixed feelings about it. On the one hand, it seemed like an incredible amount of work. On the other, it looked like less than he'd imagined. Before he'd written them down, it had felt like an infinite number of things, and now it was a big, daunting, but finite list of tasks.

When we've fallen behind, the first step is simply to list what we have to do. It's generally a lot easier to manage something on paper than in our heads. Choose activities that you need to complete in the next one to two weeks; you can apply the same principles to long-term goals at a later time. The list doesn't have to include activities of daily living—sleeping, bathing, eating, and so forth—unless you're not finding time for them.

If you've been struggling to get things done, make a list below of what you need to accomplish. At this point, don't worry about breaking the tasks into manageable pieces—that step will come later. Leave the first and last columns blank for now.

ORDER	TASKS	DUE DATE

You can find a copy of this form online at callistomediabooks.com/cbt.

Now, take a moment to review your list. What stands out? How do you feel as you look it over?

_____

_____

_____

_____

_____

_____

_____

PRIORITIZING TASKS

Walter and I returned to his list and considered where he should begin. "I want to get these Incompletes finished over spring break," he said, which meant he'd need to have them done before the end of March. We went through each item in turn and wrote the date when he needed or wanted to complete it. These dates determined the order in which he would tackle each item.

1 - Finish Incompletes - March 18
5 - Read six chapters of psych textbook - April 6
3 - Two experiments for intro psych - March 30
4 - Six math problem sets - April 2
2 - Write History paper - March 23

Return to your list of tasks. When does each one need to be completed? Write the date next to each one. Based on these dates, assign an order number to each task, with a 1 for the first one that needs to be done.

PLANNING AND COMPLETING TASKS

Based on his prioritized list, Walter knew he would first focus on his Incomplete courses. Understandably, he found the idea of "Finish Incompletes" overwhelming—"Where do I start?" he wondered. It was the same feeling that had kept him from finishing them in the first place.

So together we broke down this big task into smaller ones. We started by listing what he needed to do for each course. We broke down the larger assignments further into steps that felt doable for Walter:

Finish Incompletes:

Bio
Research paper
- Review topic and research articles
- Summarize existing studies
- Describe outstanding question
- Describe proposed answer #1
- Evidence for
- Evidence against
- Describe proposed answer #2
- Evidence for
- Evidence against
- Conclusions

History
Reflection paper one
Reflection paper two
Final paper
- Make outline
- Choose sources
- Introduction
- Section 1
- Section 2
- Conclusions

Take a look at your first activity to complete. Would it be helpful to break it into smaller pieces, or does it seem like a realistic piece to tackle the way it is? Use the space below if you need to divide the activity into smaller subtasks:

Task:

_____

Subtasks:

_____

_____

_____

_____

Use the Breaking Down Tasks form at the end of this chapter (see page 155) if you need to do the same for other items on your list.

As Walter planned to work on his Incompletes, he set dates for when he needed to complete each part of the plan, with the final due date of March 18 in mind. We did the planning on March 12, so his plan looked like this:

Finish Incompletes:

Bio   - 3/16
Research paper
• Review topic and
  research articles - 3/12
• Summarize existing studies - 3/13
• Describe outstanding question - 3/13
• Describe proposed answer #1 - 3/14
• Evidence for - 3/14
• Evidence against - 3/14
• Describe proposed answer #2 - 3/15
• Evidence for - 3/15
• Evidence against - 3/15
• Conclusions - 3/16

History   - 3/18
Reflection paper one - 3/12
Reflection paper two - 3/13
Final paper - 3/18
• Make outline - 3/14
• Choose sources - 3/14
• Introduction - 3/15
• Section 1 - 3/16
• Section 2 - 3/17
• Conclusions - 3/18

I asked Walter if this plan seemed realistic. Did he have any concerns with his ability to complete each task? We started with the plan for later that day. He had said he wanted to write a reflection paper for his history class and review his bio topic and the research articles he had chosen to include. "The paper's only one to two pages, and it's on a topic I know well, so I don't think that'll be a problem. And I just need to review the topic I chose for my bio class and look over the research articles again. So yeah, I think I can manage that."

If you divided your task(s) into subtasks, decide when you need to complete each subtask based on when your task needs to be finished, working backward from the due date for the entire task. Add the dates to the list(s) of subtasks.

The final step in the planning phase was to put the items into Walter's calendar. He worked around other commitments he had—he was going out to dinner with his family on March 17, for example—and he blocked out times he would complete each activity. At first he was reluctant to assign a specific time to each task. "That's not how I've worked in the past," he said. We talked about the pros and cons of being specific with his scheduling, and he agreed to give this new approach a try this week.

Each task you've set for yourself needs a specific time when you'll plan to complete it. Using the list you made for yourself above for your first task, find a place in your calendar when you'll complete it. If you've broken the task into subtasks, schedule times for each subtask. Repeat this process for each task on your list. You can move a task to a different time if something changes in your calendar (for example, if a new family commitment arises).

Sometimes this approach can feel overly structured, especially if you're used to a more flexible schedule. If you're feeling intimidated by this plan, consider trying it for a few days with a limited number of tasks. Plan to complete some tasks at specifically scheduled times and others in a more flexible time frame (for example, on a given day) and see how things go. This way, you'll have a basis for comparing a more versus less structured approach to task management.

Take a few moments to reflect on the process so far. How are you feeling about this approach? Write your reflections in the space below.

_____

_____

_____

_____

_____

_____

_____

_____

_____

_____

The final step is to follow the plan you set up for yourself. If you've identified, prioritized, and planned, much of the work is done by now. Over the coming week, keep careful track of when you planned to do things, and complete each task at the assigned time if at all possible. If you aren't able to complete something as planned, move it to a new time.

MISE EN PLACE

If you've ever watched a cooking show, you know the chefs have all their ingredients prepared beforehand—a process called _mise en place_ in French (pronounced "meez on ploss"). It means "putting things in place" before jumping into cooking. When it comes time to cook, the chef simply adds each ingredient at the right time. In the same way, we can practice _mise en place_ with our task management, preparing when and how we'll accomplish our tasks before carrying them out. While it takes time up front, it saves time in the long run as we can work more efficiently and with less stress.

Setting Yourself Up to Succeed

The plan for completing tasks is relatively straightforward: pick, prioritize, plan, and complete. If only it were always that easy! When we're anxious and depressed, many things can get in the way of smoothly following the plan we make for ourselves. Let's build on the general approach and incorporate strategies that set you up to succeed.

CREATE MANAGEABLE PIECES

For each task, Walter asked himself if he felt like he could do it. When we were planning his history paper, he said at one point, "I have no idea how to write this paper." He explained that the idea of WRITING A PAPER felt mammoth, like more than he could wrap his arms or his mind around.

"Do you know how to write an outline?" I asked him.

"Yes, I can do that," he said. "But I never had to in the past—I could just sort of put it together as I went along."

We talked briefly about accepting that for now, his old way of working wasn't working for him, and he agreed that he needed to break down the task. At each step I would ask him, "Do you know how to do it?" meaning, "Do you have a clear idea of how to get started?" When he didn't, we would work to break the task into even smaller pieces.

When we looked at the plan for writing his paper, he said, "I feel a little silly having it all spelled out for me like this. I mean, I've been writing papers for many years now. But it does make it seem easier."

When we're having trouble getting started, some tasks can feel like trying to get a Frisbee off a roof without a ladder. We stand staring up at the Frisbee, willing ourselves to levitate. There's nothing wrong with us for not being able to levitate; we just need a ladder. A ladder turns a 10-foot gap into a series of 1-foot gaps.

For any task you plan for yourself, see if it feels like a step you can take relatively easily. If you're struggling to complete a big project at work, for example, have you broken down the task into small enough steps that you have a clear idea of how to do each one? Or if you're behind on taking care of things at home, do you know where to begin?

Take a few moments now to think about a project you've been struggling to complete. Write it in the space below.

_____

Do you need to break it into smaller steps? If so, what would the steps look like? Write them in the spaces below.

Step 1:

_____

Step 2:

_____

Step 3:

_____

Step 4:

_____

Step 5:

_____

Step 6:

_____

Review the steps you identified. Does each one feel manageable? If necessary, break each step into smaller steps.

"I'LL TRY."

The word "try" can mean very different things, as I learned from Dr. Rob DeRubeis, one of my therapy supervisors in graduate school. The true meaning of the word according to Merriam-Webster involves effort and action. For example, people *try* to climb Mount Everest. Sometimes we say "I'll try" when we mean something closer to "I want" or "I hope," as in, "I'll try to go to the gym tomorrow." If you find yourself saying you'll try, notice if you mean it in the active sense or the wanting sense. The more active you make your trying, the more you set yourself up to succeed.

BE REALISTIC ABOUT TIMING

One of the most important steps in planning for success is to give yourself enough time to complete your tasks. It's easy to be overly optimistic about what we can accomplish in a given amount of time, and if we don't finish, or have to rush and don't do our best work, we're not going to feel good about the outcome.

As you plan your tasks, think carefully about how long each one is likely to take you. Beware not to plan for how long something "should" take, and instead plan for how long it's *likely* to take. For example, I might say to myself, "I should be able to do a grocery shop in 45 minutes." But if I think about the times I've been to the store recently, it's always taken at least an hour and 15 minutes, because I don't factor in time for standing in line and putting away the groceries at home. It's demoralizing to feel like we're always taking too long to do something. If you notice you underestimated how long things would take you, use this information the next time you schedule the task.

SET ALARMS AND REMINDERS

For any task you plan, make sure you have a nearly foolproof reminder for when to do it. "I'll just have to make sure I remember" is a recipe for forgetting. It's hard enough to "remember to remember" when we're feeling well, and even more so when we're anxious and depressed.

Different methods can work. One reliable way is to put appointments into an electronic calendar on your phone, and turn on the notification function so the phone will sound an alarm to remind you. Keep your phone nearby, with the audio turned on, so you don't miss the reminder.

Also be sure to do the task immediately when the alarm goes off. If for some reason you can't, be sure to set another reminder. If you catch yourself saying things like, "I'll just finish what I'm doing here and then get to it," stop and set another reminder. Otherwise it's a lot like not setting an alarm at all, since it's too easy to get absorbed in something else and forget to do what you'd planned.

BUILD IN ACCOUNTABILITY

"I also need to contact my academic dean," Walter told me. "She told me to keep her updated this semester, and I've been avoiding her since I fell behind." He paused. "I've also been avoiding my professors ... and my advisor. I know it's better to let them know where things stand, but it's also an unpleasant reminder that I'm not on top of things."

We made a plan for Walter to contact each of his professors that evening by e-mail. He was nervous, and we worked together to write an outline of what he needed to say. He felt like his biggest challenge was to contact his dean, whom he was somewhat afraid of. He didn't trust himself to follow through on e-mailing her, so he composed and sent the e-mail in my office.

We discussed the importance of accountability in week 2 when we addressed behavioral activation (pages 70–71). The same principles apply here. If we know someone else knows our plans, we're more likely to complete them.

When we're struggling to take care of our responsibilities, we often avoid contact with the people we feel we're letting down: professors, bosses, customers, spouses. We might tell ourselves they don't need to know what's going on until we've been able to catch up, or that because we've been out of touch for so long it's going to be incredibly uncomfortable to talk with them now. In the vast majority of cases, more is lost than gained by avoiding contact with people to whom we're accountable.

Are there people in your own life that you need to get in touch with whom you've been avoiding? If so, write who the people are in the space below.

_____

_____

_____

_____

If it's time to get in touch with these people, circle the ones you'll contact this week and write in your calendar when you'll contact them.

DECIDE TO START

Many times we prevent ourselves from starting a project because we don't know exactly how we're going to do it. For example, I've often delayed writing e-mails because I didn't know what I was going to say. However, once we *decide* to start a project, we give ourselves the opportunity to figure it out. If we wait till we know how to do the task, we may never get started, because figuring out how to do it is part of the task.

We might delay starting tasks both big and small because we don't know exactly what we're going to do. Are there tasks in your own life that you've delayed starting because you don't know how to complete them? If so, write them in the space below.

_____

_____

_____

_____

Circle any tasks that you want to start this week, and add them to your schedule.

REWARD YOURSELF

We're more likely to do things when they lead to reward. Although completing activities can be rewarding in and of itself, we can help ourselves even more by finding small rewards for meeting a goal.

A political junkie, Walter's reward to himself was pausing to read two news articles after working for 45 minutes. He got additional motivation from having something to look forward to immediately after his work. Knowing he only had to work for 45 minutes at a time also further divided his work into chunks that felt doable.

Think about ways you might give yourself small rewards for working on your tasks. Examples include snacks, entertainment, relaxation, socializing—be as creative as you need to be to find something that works for you. One caveat: Avoid activities that tend to be addictive, like playing video games or watching TV. Minimize the risk that a reward interferes with getting back on task. Also remove the reward from immediate availability once you're back to work—for example, close your Web browser, or return the cookies to the cabinet.

MAKE SPACE

Once Walter was back at school, he found it was almost impossible to work in his dorm room. His roommate was a frequent distraction, as were the other students who often stopped by. Even when he was alone with the door closed, he was pulled toward various distractions: TV, video games, music. He realized he needed to work in a quiet part of the library to be productive.

We work best when we have the space we need, both physical space and mental space. We can clear physical space by organizing our work area—whether it's an office, a desk, a kitchen, or a garage. Organization takes time up front and saves us time in the end.

Do you need to organize your work space to make it easier to get things done? Write your thoughts in the space below.

_____

_____

_____

_____

_____

We also need mental space to work well, which means eliminating unnecessary distractions. If you're working on a complicated spreadsheet, for example, consider closing your e-mail and silencing your phone so you won't be disturbed.

What tends to distract you when you're trying to be productive? Are there ways to remove the distractions from your environment? Record your thoughts below.

_____

_____

_____

_____

_____

PRACTICE ACCEPTANCE

Perhaps more than anything else, an attitude of acceptance can make a tremendous difference in taking care of what we need to do. We need to accept, first of all, that it will be difficult to follow our plan at times. The difficulty does not mean we should abandon the plan. On the contrary, things that are worthwhile tend to be difficult. Rather than retreating from difficulty, we can embrace it: "This is hard." And we can move through the difficulty, rather than running from it.

We can also accept that we'll be facing our fear and that it's uncomfortable to resist the urge to run away. We can ask ourselves, "How uncomfortable am I willing to be to do what's important to me?" Often we can suffer less simply by accepting discomfort—by no longer resisting pain, but recogizing that it will be part of what we need to do for the time being.

When you meet your edge and are tempted to avoid, what can you tell yourself to encourage acceptance of the inevitable discomfort?

_____

_____

_____

_____

_____

In the coming week, work through the activities you planned into your schedule. I also encourage you to choose two or three of the strategies for success to focus on as you work through your plan. Working on a limited number of strategies at a time can provide helpful focus as you practice what may be new skills. Write in the spaces below the strategies you plan to focus on.

1.

_____

2.

_____

3.

_____

Barriers and How to Remove Them

If you're struggling to complete tasks, several barriers often get in the way. Fortunately, the factors we've covered can be very helpful in moving past them.

I'M PROCRASTINATING

Most of us, at times, put off doing things. Sometimes we know exactly what we need to do and we wait to do it; other times we have a decision to make and we put off making it. Either way, we're procrastinating.

Are there certain tasks you routinely put off? If so, what leads you to delay doing them? How do you feel while you're procrastinating?

_____

_____

_____

_____

_____

_____

Why do we procrastinate? Usually for one of two reasons: Either we're afraid we won't do well, or we find the task aversive. Anything we can do to decrease our fear and make the task more appealing can combat procrastination.

Besides practicing several of the factors we looked at above—practicing acceptance of the fact that we're afraid, increasing our accountability, rewarding ourselves, or breaking a task into more manageable pieces—we can also address thoughts that encourage procrastination, using the tools from weeks 3 and 4. For example, we might tell ourselves that delaying is helpful in some way, or that we "just want to relax"—even though most of us don't get a lot of enjoyment out of the time we spend avoiding.

Walter recognized a theme in his thinking when he was avoiding doing something he knew he had to do. He would say to himself, "It's too hard to do it now. It'll be easier to do it later." And yet he found that it rarely got easier to do—he finally would complete the task out of desperation as the deadline was upon him. He crafted a more reality-based thought that read, "I'm probably never going to feel like doing this task, and so I may as well take care of it now rather than continue to dread it."

Are you aware of anything you tell yourself about procrastinating that may not be accurate? If so, what could you tell yourself that would be helpful?

_____

_____

_____

_____

_____

_____

_____

_____

ATTENTION DEFICIT/HYPERACTIVITY DISORDER

Problems with attention, task completion, punctuality, and procrastination are also prominent in attention deficit/hyperactivity disorder, or ADHD, according to the *DSM-5*. While many of the same techniques presented in this chapter are used in treating ADHD (see, for example, Ari Tuckman's *Integrative Treatment for Adult ADHD*), they are not intended to be stand-alone treatments for this condition. If you have ADHD as well as depression and anxiety, consider talking with a mental health professional about the best treatment approach for you.

PUNCTUALITY

Are you often late when you need to be somewhere? Punctuality is a task that involves getting yourself somewhere by a deadline, and the principles of time and task management covered in this chapter apply equally well. If you want to improve your punctuality, try using alarms and reminders, being realistic about timing, using accountability, and rewarding yourself for being on time.

I'M OVERWHELMED

When we've fallen behind, we often feel like there's more to do than we can manage. If we have in mind everything that's not done, naturally it's going to feel like too much. Practice treating your current task as if it's the only thing you have to do—because, while you're doing it, *it is* the only thing you have to do. You might even practice telling yourself, "This is the only thing I have to do right now."

Making sure each task is manageable, and knowing you've assigned each task a specific time, can also help with feeling overwhelmed. Removing unnecessary distractions from your surroundings likewise can provide more mental space to work in.

Finally, we can ask ourselves the important question: Does it all have to get done? When you find yourself saying or feeling *I have to do this*, you can ask yourself, "Do I really? What would happen if I didn't?" Sometimes the answer will be, "Yes, in fact, I *do* really need to do this." Other times we might decide that, as much as we'd *like* to complete something, it's not worth the cost to our well-being.

I HAVE NO MOTIVATION

Motivation tends to be low either because the task is unappealing or we lack the drive to complete it. It's like our foot is stuck on the brake and our accelerator isn't working. We can take our foot off the brake by making the task less unpleasant—by doing things like breaking it down into manageable pieces. We can also engage our accelerator by making the task more rewarding, like by giving ourselves small incentives for doing it. Thankfully, motivation builds as we gain momentum.

What have you found increases your motivation to complete tasks?

_____

_____

_____

_____

_____

I SHOULD JUST BE ABLE TO DO THIS

At times, we might resist using time and task management strategies to help us take care of our responsibilities. We might tell ourselves things like, "This shouldn't be this hard," or, "I'm just going to force myself to do it."

A mind-set of acceptance is very helpful in this regard. When we accept that things are the way they are, we open ourselves to using the tools that will help us get unstuck.

Do you notice any misgivings of your own about using the tools presented in this chapter to help you get things done? Write down what you think it means if you rely on these kinds of strategies.

_____

_____

_____

_____

_____

In this chapter, we began with a review of the techniques from previous weeks. We then built on these techniques and covered a general outline for getting things done. We also looked at ways to increase the chances of completing our tasks, as well as how to remove common barriers. Finishing the tasks we set for ourselves can play a big role in reducing our anxiety and depression. As our anxiety and depression decrease, it gets even easier to take care of things.

Take a few moments to consider how things are going for you at this point, now five weeks into this program. What's going well? Are there areas where you continue to struggle? Include any reactions to the material presented in this chapter. I'll see you in week 6, where we'll work together on facing your fears.

_____

_____

_____

_____

_____

_____

_____

_____

_____

_____

_____

_____

ACTIVITY PLAN

1 Schedule and complete your five activities.
2 Complete at least one Challenging Your Thoughts form.
3 Complete the tasks you scheduled for this week.
4 Choose two to three strategies from this week to implement.
5 Plan a time to complete week 6.

Breaking down tasks

Task: _____

    Sub-tasks: _____

                   _____

                   _____

                   _____

Task: _____

    Sub-tasks: _____

                   _____

                   _____

                   _____

Task: _____

    Sub-tasks: _____

                   _____

                   _____

                   _____

Task: _____

    Sub-tasks: _____

                   _____

                   _____

You can find a copy of this form online at callistomediabooks.com/cbt.

Facing Your Fears

Last week, we addressed time and task management, including a structured plan for getting things done as well as ways to overcome common barriers.

We're now ready to tackle the final major task for this program: how to face your fears. But first, let's revisit some familiar themes from previous chapters, as we see how things went over the past week.

You had three main goals for last week: continuing to complete enjoyable and important activities, addressing problematic thoughts, and working on ways to manage your time and tasks.

Hopefully, by now, you're on a roll with your activity completion. If you continue to struggle, return to week 2 and review the principles as needed. In the space below, briefly review your successes and any challenges in this area from the past week.

_____

_____

_____

_____

_____

Over the coming week, continue to complete activities from your list. If there are some 3s you haven't gotten to, consider adding them to your schedule. Also, choose three days to monitor your activities using the Daily Activities form (page 66).

In the past week, did you catch yourself thinking things that weren't supported by facts? Record the kinds of thoughts you noticed and challenged in the space below.

_____

_____

_____

_____

_____

_____

_____

By now, you may be at a point where you can begin to dismiss thoughts more efficiently, without going through the full evidence-finding exercise. It's usually helpful to have something to say in response to the thoughts. For example, in week 4, we saw how Alex, when she caught herself having an inaccurate thought, would say things like, "Someone's lying about me again." Other possibilities include:

1 "There go my thoughts."
2 "Okay, back to reality."
3 "Thank goodness _that's_ not true."
4 "Not everything you think is true."

The options are endless—just find something that resonates with you. In the coming week, continue to notice if and when your thoughts aren't helping you. If you can't easily dismiss a troubling thought, plan to complete a Challenging Your Thoughts form for it.

If you planned to complete some tasks using specific strategies for time and task management, how well did you follow the plan you laid out for yourself? Did anything go worse than expected, or better? If you struggled to stick to the plan you set for yourself, what got in the way?

_____

_____

_____

_____

_____

_____

_____

_____

_____

_____

_____

_____

_____

_____

_____

_____

If you found yourself struggling, consider reviewing week 5. You might return to the section on barriers and see if any of them apply. If so, review possible ways to remove barriers.

In the coming week, continue to follow the plan for listing, prioritizing, and scheduling your tasks. It can take repeated attempts to push through avoidance and start being more productive. Practice being patient with yourself as you find what works for you.

Facing Fears

"I realize that, in some way, this fear has affected every part of my life."

Julie first experienced social anxiety in seventh grade. Now 27 years old, she's been struggling with it for more than half her life. As she tells me all the social situations she's afraid of, it's a little hard to square with the confident and articulate young woman with a quick sense of humor who is sitting in front of me. I tell her as much.

"It's not everywhere," she tells me. "I know you're not going to judge me. It's whenever I'm talking with someone who might think I'm stupid or awkward." She pauses, then continues. "The weird thing is, I know I'm not stupid or awkward. I mean, I know it now. But as soon as I'm around someone new, or I have to speak in front of a group, or I'm on a date, I seize up. It's like the spotlight's on me, someone hands me a mic, and I forgot to prepare my speech."

She's been working since college at a tech start-up, and she's been recognized for doing good work. Kevin, the senior member of her team, has let her know he's impressed with her innovative ideas, and encouraged her to speak up about them in their team meetings. Try as she might, Julie can't bring herself to volunteer her ideas in front of the team. She was mortified when Kevin asked her why she didn't give her input more in meetings, and she had to admit that she struggles with confidence when speaking in a group. She can feel him looking at her now in meetings when he asks if "anyone else has any suggestions." She often feels caught between his gentle but persistent pressure to speak, and her paralyzing social anxiety.

Recently, Kevin told her he wants to recommend her for an exciting new project, but he's concerned about her ability to lead a group. Julie is secretly relieved—she has major concerns about leading a group, especially the talking-in-front-of-the-group part. At the same time, she wants to move up in her field, and it would be a great opportunity. Besides, she's not dating, also because of her social anxiety, so she could use a bigger challenge at work. Once again, she feels trapped: between wanting to avoid social situations that terrify her and being stuck at a level below her potential.

In this chapter, we'll address how to face fears like the ones Julie has. While she struggles with social anxiety, the principles we'll cover apply to all types of fears.

The techniques we'll focus on are based on the principle that the most effective way to overcome our fear is to expose ourselves to the situations that trigger it. Thus, this treatment approach is called exposure. Exposure therapy is used for facing situations we truly fear.

If you struggle with major fears, the cognitive work you've done so far will be helpful. Challenging the validity of our fears can be a crucial step toward facing them. It's unlikely to get rid of our fears, but once we realize our fears probably aren't warranted, we tend to be more willing to confront them directly.

Take a moment to think about your own fears. Write in the space below what your main fears are. Do these fears get in the way of living your life to the fullest?

Principles of Facing Fears

In the first few sessions, Julie and I developed a plan for moving toward her goals. We examined the thoughts she had about social situations—especially the predictions she made for how things would go in specific encounters. Over time, she realized there was probably not as much to fear as she thought. For instance, she didn't judge people harshly even when they did something a little foolish, so she had little reason to assume others were being highly critical of her.

At this point it was time for Julie to face her fears directly. We began by reviewing the principles of facing our fears. Why do something that we know is going to make us uncomfortable?

ANXIETY GOES DOWN

If we felt just as scared every time we faced our fears, it'd be hard to make the case for doing so. Why suffer if we don't have to? Fear is based on an expectation that something is dangerous. When we face a scary situation and nothing bad actually happens, our brains acquire new information about that situation. This way, when we face our fears, they diminish. Generally, we don't have to talk ourselves into being less afraid—just by doing what we're afraid of, it gets easier.

For example, I used to have a big fear of spiders. One fall, a large orb-weaving spider built its web in the door frame of my garage. Every morning, I'd pass the spider on my way through the garage. The first few times I saw it, I was really nervous and walked past it as quickly as possible, half expecting it to jump on me. Over a few weeks, I came to fear the spider less, and eventually even felt friendly toward it. I was actually sorry when it stopped building its web there and I never saw it again. After that experience, I was no longer so afraid of spiders when I'd see them.

Think of a time you faced your fears and they diminished, and write about it in the space below.

_____

_____

_____

_____

_____

WORKING THROUGH ANXIETY, FROM THE GROUND UP

Years ago, I provided treatment for Ron, a middle-aged man dealing with panic attacks. When I described the process of gradually confronting our fears, he gave me a metaphor that stuck with me.

Ron had had a fear of heights when he was a younger man. When he was in his twenties, he was working construction in a small town where most of the buildings were only two or three stories tall, so his fear of heights was not much of an issue. When he moved to a city, where the jobs were bigger, he knew he'd be working on taller buildings and worried he might not be able to do it.

One of his first jobs was helping to build a 16-story building. Ron was sure he'd have to find a different project to work on. But thankfully for Ron, buildings are built from the ground up. In the beginning, he was working belowground as the foundation went in, then on the ground level in the weeks that followed. When they began work on the second floor, he was a little nervous but got used to it fairly quickly.

The third floor wasn't much worse than the second, and soon he was comfortable working at that height. "By the time the building was halfway up, I knew I was going to be fine," Ron told me. "It did take some getting used to each time we'd go up a little higher, but I'd had enough experience to know I'd be okay by the second or third day. Now I don't really worry about heights."

Ron's experience is a perfect application of exposure. What principles do you recognize that made his "treatment" effective?

When Facing Fears, Use Common Sense

Naturally, the process of facing our fears is helpful only for things that aren't truly dangerous. Approaching an angry stinging insect or venomous snake would not provide a positive learning experience! Keep in mind: The activities you choose should be relatively safe. While there's a certain level of risk involved in any activity (even getting out of bed in the morning), the things you choose should not present more danger than our normal day-to-day activities.

MAKE IT PROGRESSIVE

Julie decided that the only way she was going to get to a better place was to face her fears directly. We developed a list of social situations Julie was afraid of, and rated each one for how much anxiety she would experience while doing it (on a scale from 0 to 10). The activities ranged from things she was doing already to ones that were difficult for her to imagine doing. We then arranged her activities into a hierarchy; an abbreviated version looked like this:

ACTIVITY	DISTRESS LEVEL (0–10)
Giving a presentation at work	9
Going on a date	8
Going out with friends from work	7
Speaking up in team meetings	6
Going to a movie with a friend	5
Telling supervisor my ideas	4
Making conversation with grocery cashier	2

As you can see from her hierarchy, Julie's activities range from low to high anxiety (from bottom to top), and there are no big jumps between levels. Ideally, we want to create a hierarchy like a ladder, with rungs that are relatively evenly spaced.

Think again about your own fears. What are some activities that would allow you to face them incrementally? Write your thoughts below.

DO IT ON PURPOSE

"I understand the idea of exposure," Julie told me as we were planning which activities to begin with, "but why am I afraid of the things I'm already doing? I mean, it's not like I never talk in group meetings, and I tell my supervisor my ideas."

"Can you tell me about a time recently when you spoke in a group meeting?" I asked.

"Sure," she said, "Kevin asked each of us to give an update on how our project was going. When my turn came, I was really nervous, but I said what I had to and felt like I did an okay job."

"Is that how it usually goes?" I asked her. "When you speak up, is it usually because you have to, or do you do it voluntarily?"

She thought about it and said, "I guess it's pretty much only when I'm really expected to. I mean, I don't tend to say things out of the blue. I'd be afraid people would think it was a dumb idea and that I should've just kept it to myself."

Julie's example raises an important point: Exposure needs to be done on purpose to be most effective. Intentionally defying our desire to avoid our fears sends a powerful message to our brains: Maybe we don't have to be so afraid. After all, how bad can it be if I'm facing it deliberately? *Choosing* to face our fears is more effective than facing them against our will or with limited choice in the matter. For these reasons, exposure is never something that can be done *to* us, like forcing a person to touch a snake.

Consider times when you encountered the things you're afraid of without trying to. How helpful was it in reducing your fear?

_____

_____

_____

_____

_____

_____

_____

_____

Repeat as Needed

"I did it." Julie told me the following week. "I went out with some of my coworkers and it went pretty well. None of the major disasters I was afraid of actually happened."

"Great," I said. "What did you learn from this experience?"

"Well, maybe I shouldn't be so nervous in these situations. But then again, it was only one time and maybe I just got lucky. Maybe with a different mix of people, or different topics of conversation, or if I'm feeling tired, it could go really badly."

As Julie found, doing something one time is an act of courage, but it's not therapy. The therapy comes in repeating the activities until we start to feel more comfortable doing them.

Our nervous systems usually don't stop being afraid of a situation after facing it one time, and for good reason. We've all probably done something dangerous one time and gotten away with it, and realized immediately after how lucky we were. It takes repetition to dampen our fears.

Additionally, our repeated exposures need to be relatively close together in time. For example, many people are afraid of flying. If they have family far away, they may fly once a year for the holidays. Repeating an exposure (in this case, flying) once per year is typically not enough to make any difference in our level of fear. Flying several times relatively close together in time can make a big difference.

STAY THROUGH THE DISCOMFORT

"What happened this week when you went out with friends from work?" I asked Julie.

"There were a few moments when I really wanted to get out of there. I went to the bathroom at one point and thought, 'You could just slip out the back door. Probably no one would even notice.'"

"What stopped you?" I asked.

She smiled. "Well for one, I knew we'd have this conversation, and I didn't want to say I ran away. And more than that, I'm tired of running away. I've been running from my fears, but I'm also running away from life. How am I ever going to meet someone and fall in love if I can't get through this fear?"

Because Julie stayed, she found that she didn't have to escape when things got tough. She also saw that her wave of anxiety passed. In the past she'd always thought that escaping the situation was her only way to relieve her distress.

As we work through our hierarchy, it's important that we stay in a situation long enough to learn something new. If we run away at the first feeling of discomfort, we'll be reinforcing our avoidance behavior and the belief that had we stayed, things could have been really bad. It's nice if our fear goes down during the exposure itself, although, as recent research by Michelle Craske and others has shown, it doesn't have to for the exercise to be helpful.

Are there situations you've fled because you had a spike in your anxiety? What do you think would've happened had you stayed?

_____

_____

_____

_____

_____

_____

ELIMINATE UNNECESSARY PROPS

"I'm realizing how much of what I've been doing isn't necessary," Julie told me. "For instance, I always thought I had to type out a draft of what I was going to say in our team meetings. I'd go over it beforehand and memorize it as best I could. But then when I was talking, I'd either read what I'd written, which didn't make me sound very dynamic, or I'd try to remember it and get flustered if I forgot."

Julie described other things she would do to prevent her fears from coming true; for example, when she got together with friends, she preferred to go to a movie instead of dinner to avoid the possibility of "awkward silences."

I asked her what she's learned from letting go of some of these behaviors.

"I feel like Dumbo!" she said. I looked at her quizzically, and she continued. "He could fly because he had huge ears, but he thought he could fly because of the

'magic feather' his friends gave him. All these props were my 'magic feathers,' and like Dumbo, if I dropped my feather, I thought I was sunk, like when I couldn't remember the words I'd memorized. Now I can speak up in a meeting and just do my best, and so far it's gone fine."

What Julie was describing—her "magic feathers"—have been called "safety behaviors," because they're intended to "protect us" in situations where we're anxious. As Julie discovered, most of the time these behaviors are not necessary, and they can even be detrimental. For example, a man might memorize a list of questions to ask his date in case there's a lull in the conversation. Instead of having a natural conversation, he might end up cutting off interesting topics of conversation and asking a series of non sequiturs.

Even when safety behaviors don't lead to negative results, they can still come with a cost: We can tell ourselves that *things might have gone very badly if I hadn't done those things.* In this way, we prevent ourselves from learning that we can face our fears without additional props.

Think about your own feared situations and things you might do to prevent what you're afraid of from happening. Do any of these behaviors strike you as unnecessary safety behaviors that you could consider dropping? Record your thoughts in the space below.

_____

_____

_____

_____

_____

_____

_____

EMBRACE DISCOMFORT AND UNCERTAINTY

"How'd your presentation go?" I asked Julie. She had worked up to the highest item on her hierarchy, which involved giving a presentation about her team's project in front of the entire firm.

"Worse than I expected," she told me, "and yet better than I expected." She continued, "I thought it was just going to be the people in our firm. But, before the meeting, Kevin pulled me aside and told me it was also going to be a kind of dog-and-pony show for current and potential investors. I didn't realize I was basically going to be pitching a project for funding. So my anxiety was worse than I'd expected—if there was an 11 on the scale, I'd have been there."

"So how'd it go?" I asked her.

"I just decided to treat it as an opportunity, and to lean into the anxiety instead of trying to make it go away. And really, what was I gonna do? Not give the presentation? So I just said to myself, 'This is not a comfortable situation for me, and I have no idea how it's going to go. Let's see where this takes me.' And it went all right. I was terrified at first, but it got easier as I went along. And it looks like we'll have new investors for the project."

When we do what we're afraid of, it's almost certainly going to be uncomfortable. We can resist that discomfort, or we can choose to embrace it. When we accept that it's going to be scary, the fear has less power over us. It will be uncomfortable—no better, and no worse. Just uncomfortable.

We can lean into uncertainty just as we lean into discomfort. Rather than backing away from unknowns, we can tell ourselves, "I don't know what will happen, and I'm willing to do it anyway."

When you're facing your own fears, how can you encourage yourself to endure the inevitable discomfort, and to accept the inherent uncertainty? Examples include:

- Reminding yourself it will be hard, and why you're willing to do it anyway.
- Fostering an attitude of curiosity toward the experience: "Let's see how this goes."
- Keeping in mind what motivated you to face your fears in the first place.
- Remembering that discomfort doesn't last forever.
- Tapping into your sources of strength.
- Knowing that few great things are achieved through avoidance.

In the space below, write what you'll remind yourself of when tempted to pull back from facing uncertain or uncomfortable situations.

_____

_____

_____

_____

_____

_____

_____

_____

_____

_____

What Is Courage?

"Courage is not the absence of fear, but rather the judgment that something else is more important than one's fear."

—Ambrose Redmoon

Tailoring Exposure for Different Fears

While the general principles of exposure therapy hold for various types of anxiety, we can increase its effectiveness by adapting it for specific conditions.

SPECIFIC PHOBIAS

Exposure for specific phobias tends to be the most straightforward. In many cases, a single extended exposure session can effectively treat the condition. For example, one study found that, for 90 percent of people who did the treatment, about two hours of exposure led to lasting improvement or even complete recovery. The protocol can also be effective when done without therapist assistance.

Exposures for phobias should allow you to test the assumptions you have about what will happen when you interact with the thing or situation you fear. For example, if you're afraid you'll get stuck in an elevator, riding an elevator allows you to test that prediction.

If you struggle with a phobia, what do you think will happen if you confront it?

_____

_____

_____

_____

_____

_____

_____

_____

Keep these predictions in mind. They'll come in handy when you make your own exposure hierarchy later in this chapter.

PANIC DISORDER

There are many ways exposure therapy can play a role in managing panic disorder. We'll start with the easiest one: Keep breathing.

Keep Breathing. The breath is intimately connected to our nervous systems. When we're feeling calm and relaxed, our breathing tends to be slow and steady. When we're afraid, we take rapid, shallow breaths. Take a few rapid, shallow breaths now and notice how you feel. Then take a few slow breaths and see what happens.

When we're having frequent panic attacks, we tend to breathe in a way that increases physiological arousal and anxiety. By practicing a few minutes of relaxed breathing each day, we can lower our stress level. If you're working to manage panic, plan to spend five minutes per day breathing in the following way:

1 **Inhale slowly for a count of four.** It's more important that the breath be *slow* than *deep*. Breathe into the belly as much as possible, rather than the chest. Belly breathing will improve with practice.
2 **Exhale slowly for a count of four.**
3 **Pause for a count of two to four before your next inhale.**

You can also use this breathing technique during your exposure exercises. When we're facing a challenging situation and are worried about panicking, it can feel like we have no control over the situation. One thing we *can* control is where we focus our attention, and we can use the breath as a focal point to help us face our challenges.

Keep in mind that the point of the breathing is to help you through your exposure, not to take away your anxiety or make sure you don't panic. If we use the breathing as a means to "keep from panicking," it can backfire and lead to more anxiety. Remember: *The point of focusing on the breath is to focus on the breath.*

Testing Your Predictions. If you have panic disorder, hopefully at this point you've reassessed some of your beliefs about panic. For example, we might think a panic attack can lead to suffocation or "going crazy," when in fact a panic attack is not dangerous (just very distressing). We can further test our beliefs about panic through exposure exercises.

What are some of the beliefs you have about what will happen if you panic? Have some of these fears been hard to counter simply through challenging your thoughts? For example, do you expect something bad to happen (other than the panic itself)?

_____

_____

_____

_____

_____

When you design your exposure hierarchy, think about the beliefs you have and how you might test them.

Facing Our Fear of Fear. In panic disorder, we often start to fear our own bodies' reactions because they've become associated with panic. For example, we might start to fear having a fast heartbeat because our hearts race during panic; as a consequence, we might start avoiding activities that raise our heart rates, which further reinforces our fear.

Like any activity we avoid out of fear, we can practice approaching physical symptoms to decrease the discomfort they bring. This type of exercise is called interoceptive exposure; common activities and the symptoms they provoke include:

ACTIVITY	SENSATIONS
Breathing through a coffee stirrer for 1 minute	Feelings of suffocation
Running vigorously for 1 minute	Racing/pounding heart; shortness of breath
Taking 10 fast, deep breaths	Hyperventilation; numbness in extremities; feeling "unreal"
Spinning in swivel chair	Dizziness

Have you developed any fears of bodily sensations related to panic? If so, which physical sensations are uncomfortable for you to experience? Write them in the space below, as well as activities that could produce those sensations.

_____

_____

_____

_____

_____

_____

_____

_____

_____

_____

_____

If you've become afraid of physical sensations, plan to include these activities in your hierarchy.

Opening to Panic. Trying not to panic often has the paradoxical effect of creating more panic. For many people, the most powerful antidote to panic is being willing to panic. Some people even describe a mind-set of "Bring it on." When we're willing to have a panic attack, it makes us dread panic less—*and* it makes a panic attack less likely.

Being willing to bring on panic-like symptoms through interoceptive exposure is in line with this mentality. You can also practice opening to specific symptoms you experience. For example, if your heart starts to race, let it—perhaps even willing it to beat faster. Most people I've worked with find this practice quite challenging because it goes against our natural impulse to try to make panic stop. At the same time, they tend to find it very helpful.

SOCIAL ANXIETY DISORDER

CBT for social anxiety disorder includes customized techniques to address the specific cognitive components of the condition.

Using Exposures to Test Beliefs. *Julie was afraid that people would be terribly bored and uncomfortable during her presentation. We worked to identify how she would know they were feeling these things—what would they be doing? How would it differ from their behavior when others were speaking to the group?*

During her presentation, Julie forced herself to look up and see how people were responding, even though she was afraid of what she would see. To her pleasant surprise, her coworkers looked about the same as ever. Some were checking their phones, some were listening intently, others were nodding. Being specific about what she expected to see and then comparing her prediction to what actually happened allowed for a fair test of Julie's beliefs. She concluded that her fears were unfounded in this case, and probably in others.

If you'll be doing exposures for social anxiety, be sure to specify what you're afraid will happen and how you'll test whether it did. It's easy to rely on our gut feeling about how things went. If we're prone to a lot of social anxiety, our gut will be biased to believe we did badly.

Consider a social situation you fear and what you're afraid might happen when you confront it. How could you set up an exposure to test your predictions?

_____

_____

_____

_____

_____

_____

_____

Dropping Safety Behaviors. *"I'm finding I don't have to do as much in social situations as I thought I had to,"* Julie told me. *"Like when I'd go out with friends, I'd constantly be thinking of what I was going to say next. I was so worried about any awkward pause in the conversation."*

"What's it been like as you've let go of some of those things?" I asked her.

"Well I was surprised at first that the conversation didn't come to a screeching halt. I'd been doing it for so long, I just assumed it was the only thing between me and these terrible silences." She paused. *"I guess I really feel like I'm in the conversation now. Before I was maybe one-quarter in it and three-quarters in my head, so I wasn't really hearing the other person. I was so focused on making sure I had something to say."*

Julie went on to say that one of her friends recently told her she really enjoyed talking with her because Julie was such a good listener. Julie was starting to see that she was a valued friend, not the socially awkward person others wanted to avoid like she'd assumed.

Julie found that, by dropping her safety behaviors (see page 168), she was able to be herself more and be more present for others. Letting go of safety behaviors is especially important in social anxiety disorder because they can actually worsen our social abilities, as well as lead us to believe we can't do well without them. Other examples of safety behaviors in social anxiety disorder include:

- Keeping my hands in my pockets so people don't see them shake
- Excessively rehearsing what I'm going to say before speaking
- Asking lots of questions to avoid talking about myself
- Relying on alcohol to relax in social situations

If you struggle with social anxiety, can you identify any of your own safety behaviors in social situations? What do you think are the advantages of using these behaviors? The disadvantages?

_____

_____

_____

_____

_____

_____

Turning Attention Outward. *As Julie prepared to do her exposures, we talked about where her attention is in social situations. "I'm usually checking to see how I'm doing," she said. "If I'm paying attention to the other person, it's often to try to see if I'm making them uncomfortable." She laughed. "That's probably why I never remember people's names when we're introduced—I'm just trying to see if this person thinks I'm weird!"*

As we discussed it further, Julie realized focusing on herself only increases her anxiety, which makes her more self-conscious, which leads to even greater anxiety. "What would happen if you stopped focusing on yourself during conversations?" I asked her.

"I don't know," she said. "It might go better. But I also worry I'll be acting weird and making people feel awkward and I won't know it." She agreed to practice taking the spotlight off herself in her social interactions and see what would happen.

Self-focus can be thought of as a type of safety behavior. Like other safety behaviors, it probably doesn't help us and likely makes things worse.

When you're in uncomfortable social situations, how much of your attention is directed toward yourself and how you're coming across, versus on the other person? If you find yourself being focused on yourself, what effects have you noticed?

_____

_____

_____

_____

_____

_____

_____

_____

During your exposures for social anxiety, practice directing your attention away from yourself and what others think of you. You might choose to focus instead on the person you're talking with and what they are saying, or on *being in* the conversation, presentation, or whatever you're doing, rather than *monitoring* how you're doing.

GENERALIZED ANXIETY DISORDER (GAD)

Most of the fears we've focused on so far have been about things that are unlikely to happen—our plane crashing, for example—or that wouldn't be as bad as we think, like blushing in front of a group. When our anxiety is focused mainly on worries, our fear is based on our lack of control over the things we care about most.

For example, we worry about our children's safety, or losing our parents, or our job security, or being in a major car accident—anything that would involve tremendous disappointment, suffering, or loss. Even if we don't meet all the criteria for GAD, almost all of us worry more than we need to about things we can't control.

Do you find yourself repeatedly worrying about things? If so, list some of your recent worries in the space below.

_____

_____

_____

_____

_____

_____

_____

_____

Worry as Avoidance. It's hard to make an exposure hierarchy for worries; by definition, the anxiety in generalized anxiety disorder isn't confined to a specific set of situations or objects. Additionally, avoidance may not be as apparent as in conditions like panic disorder or specific phobia. Nevertheless, there is a version of exposure that can be helpful for the worry and _cognitive_ avoidance—the effort to push certain fears out of one's mind—that are part of GAD.

The act of worrying itself can be an attempt (usually unintentional) to avoid thinking about really frightening things that could happen. For example, if we're terrified of losing our job and becoming homeless, our minds might cling to worries about things we have more control over, like getting to work on time. If we're afraid of losing our aging parents, we might focus our worries on making sure they take their medication. In the process, our minds are doing their best to push away the really scary image of being homeless, burying a parent, and other frightening prospects.

The problem with pushing things out of our minds is that they tend to come back more often. In one classic study by Daniel Wegner and his fellow researchers, participants were told not to think of a white bear during a five-minute period. Of course, the harder they tried not to think about it, the more often they did.

Accepting What We Fear. When we run from what we fear, it can make what we're afraid of seem worse than bad. There's something about confronting our worries head-on that can make them less threatening. Thus, the antidote for avoiding thinking about our fears is to deliberately think about them. When we have worries about bad things happening, we can practice exposing ourselves mentally to the possibility that what we're afraid of could happen.

For example, if I worry that I might get sick and miss a big family trip I've been looking forward to, my worries about missing the trip might lead me to think of everything I can do to avoid getting sick: wash my hands, get adequate sleep, avoid people who are sick, and so forth. By worrying about these more mundane matters, I can push away the thought that I could miss the trip.

Despite my best efforts, though, there's no way to be sure I won't miss the trip. As a result, my mind will continue to ask, "What if you get sick?" as the trip approaches. In this case, I could practice accepting the possibility that what I'm afraid of might happen: "It's possible that I'll get sick and miss the trip, and be really sad I wasn't with my family for this special occasion," I could tell myself.

Most likely, we'll have an initial increase in anxiety from telling ourselves that what we fear might happen. However, if we continue to practice responding to our worries with acceptance, they tend to lose their sting and stop bothering us as much.

If you're prone to worry that's hard to control, what are some statements that would help you practice accepting the uncertainty surrounding what you fear?

_____

_____

_____

_____

_____

_____

Living in an Imaginary Future. When we worry about events that might happen—like losing our health or our loved ones—we can feel as though these events have already happened. In doing so, we suffer many times over, even before a challenging event has occurred.

For example, if we dwell on an image of ourselves being stuck in a nursing home, lonely and depressed, we'll spend a lot of time feeling bad about something that might never happen.

Can you think of a recent time when you were so worried about something that you felt like it was happening already? If so, describe it in the space below.

_____

_____

_____

_____

_____

_____

_____

_____

_____

_____

I like to pair accepting the possibility that what we worry about could happen with *a return to the present*, to what's actually going on. That way, we neither run from our worries nor give them more airtime than they deserve.

When you catch yourself worrying, practice acknowledging that what you're afraid of could happen. Then, turn your attention back to whatever you're doing. It can be helpful to focus on sensory experiences: what you see, hear, smell, feel, and/or taste.

Keep in mind that the point of returning to the present is not to avoid our fears, but to be more fully engaged in the reality of our lives.

Creating Your Own Hierarchy

Now it's time to put together your own exposure hierarchy. If you prefer, you can make your hierarchy in a spreadsheet so the items are easy to sort by difficulty level. If you want to use paper and pen, fill in the form below.

Review the notes you've taken throughout this chapter to develop items that will be a part of your hierarchy. Keep in mind that you don't have to be able to do all of them at this time. As you work your way up, the more difficult ones will start to feel more doable.

For the anxiety scale, use the following guidelines. Note that the absolute numbers are not that important; they just allow you to rank the difficulty of the activities.

> 0 = No Distress;
> 5 = Difficult but Manageable;
> 10 = Most Distress I've Ever Felt

The hierarchy form includes reminders of the key points to make your exposure successful. There are additional spaces at the bottom so you can add any other reminders you want to include for yourself. For example, you might include a reminder of what's more important than your fear.

EXPOSURE HIERARCHY

ACTIVITY	DISTRESS LEVEL (0–10)

Reminders:

- Anxiety goes down when we face it.
- Work through your hierarchy progressively and systematically.
- Stay through discomfort.
- Eliminate unnecessary props and safety behaviors.
- Embrace discomfort and uncertainty.
- _____
- _____
- _____

You can find a copy of this form online at callistomediabooks.com/cbt.

Planning Items to Complete

Review your exposure hierarchy. Where is a good starting point for you? Plan to start with activities that will be difficult but manageable. You'll want to set yourself up to succeed, so choose activities you're confident you can do. At the same time, if you have items ranked 1 or 2, you might want to pick something a bit more challenging so you make the best use of your time. If you prefer to arrange the activities in order from easier to harder, reorder your activities on a blank exposure hierarchy form.

Choose two to three of the activities that you feel you can complete this week, and write them in the spaces below.

Activity 1:

_____

Activity 2:

_____

Activity 3:

_____

As with any activity you intend to complete, choose a time to do each one and add them to your calendar.

If you've planned to complete activities you're afraid of, this is a big day: You are on your way to conquering your fears.

You've now worked through six modules of this self-directed treatment. Congratulations on all the work you've done. Next week, we'll review what you've done as we put all the pieces together. You'll have the opportunity to take stock of the ground you've covered, the progress you've made, and the work you still need to do.

For now, take a few moments to consider how you're feeling in week 6 of this program. What stands out to you from this chapter on facing your fears? Record your thoughts and feelings in the space below.

_____

_____

_____

_____

_____

_____

_____

_____

_____

_____

_____

ACTIVITY PLAN

1 Continue completing your scheduled activities from your Getting Back to Life list.
2 Monitor your activities for three days using the Daily Activities form.
3 Be aware of your thinking, especially when you have a surge of negative emotion, and complete a Challenging Your Thoughts form as needed.
4 Continue completing tasks from week 5.
5 Complete the first few items from your exposure hierarchy at the times you planned.
6 Schedule a time to complete week 7.

Putting It All Together

At this point, we've covered all the topics included in this workbook. We'll devote most of this chapter to integrating all the pieces. We'll also discuss a plan to move forward as you wrap up this seven-week program.

Last week we focused on ways to tame your fears, working progressively through a plan to confront them. Before we talk about how to best integrate all the pieces, let's review how things went as you started that process.

If you worked on confronting your fears over the past week, take a few moments to consider how things went. What went well with your exposures? Where did you find yourself struggling?

_____

_____

_____

_____

_____

_____

_____

_____

If you had a hard time completing your planned exposures, take heart—many people have a hard time at first, and the vast majority go on to do very well. Review the principles of what makes exposure effective, and choose a more approachable starting point. You might also remind yourself what compelled you to face your fear—what, on the other side, makes the difficulty worthwhile?

_____

_____

_____

_____

_____

_____

Part of the activity plan from last week included monitoring your activities for three days. Take a look at your Daily Activities forms for this week. How do they compare to the Daily Activities forms you completed between weeks 1 and 2? Is there a difference in the overall level of activity? Also examine the Enjoyment and Importance columns: Do you notice any changes? Write your observations below.

_____

_____

_____

_____

_____

_____

_____

_____

_____

Continue to do activities from your list, reviewing week 2 as needed.

You've been paying attention to the things your mind tells you for the past four weeks. What do you find helpful about this approach?

_____

_____

_____

_____

_____

Over the past week, did you notice thoughts that seemed especially important to examine carefully? If so, describe the thoughts and your process of questioning them below.

_____

_____

_____

_____

_____

Are there ongoing challenges you're finding in recognizing and addressing your problematic patterns of thinking? If so, describe them in the space below.

_____

_____

_____

_____

_____

Continue to review weeks 3 and 4 as needed, to address issues that come up and to reinforce the material.

How did completing the tasks you scheduled for yourself go over the past week?

_____

_____

_____

_____

_____

If you've continued to struggle with getting things done, what has gotten in your way?

_____

_____

_____

_____

You can review the material in week 5 as needed to address ongoing challenges in this area. Remember to follow the plan closely, especially if you run into difficulty doing your tasks.

Looking Back

"When I first came here, I thought I was going crazy. Everything seemed to be falling apart, and I felt like I was drowning." John had completed the acute part of his treatment, and we had decided together to cut back our meetings to once every three weeks. In preparation, we reviewed how the treatment had gone for him thus far.

When John called me to discuss treatment options, I recognized his name but couldn't place it. Then I realized I'd seen it on the fleet of plumbing trucks that bore his name driving around the suburbs. John's anxiety had grown with his business, as he realized he was responsible not only for his own family, but for the families of his employees.

Every day, he listened with dread to his work voice mail, fearing the call about a major plumbing disaster his company would be responsible for. He'd been spending more and more time at work, much of it worrying and not really being productive. He felt terrible about being away from home as much as he was, and not being as present as a father and husband as he wanted to be. When he was home, he was rarely there mentally, as he worried and ruminated about work. He'd stopped spending time with the close group of friends he'd known since elementary school and given up exercise and reading for pleasure. During our first session, he'd told me, "Most of my time I spend working, worrying about work, and feeling guilty for working."

Based on his life picture at the time, John's goals were:

- *Find balance between work life and home life.*
- *Worry less about things I can't control.*
- *Be more productive at work.*
- *Find time for things that bring me joy.*

At the start of this seven-week program, you took an inventory of how things were going in different areas of your life. Based on that inventory, you developed specific goals to work toward. Look back at your list of goals. For each one, think about the progress you've made and record your impressions in the space below.

_____

_____

_____

_____

_____

_____

_____

_____

_____

Later in this chapter we'll discuss ways to keep moving toward your goals.

John and I had used a CBT framework to understand his situation. At the beginning of treatment, his thoughts, emotions, and behaviors were working against him in a self-perpetuating cycle:

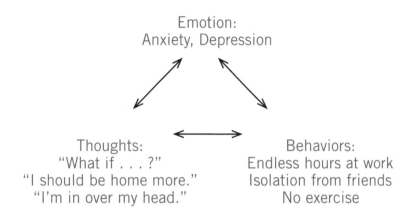

Emotion:
Anxiety, Depression

Thoughts:
"What if . . . ?"
"I should be home more."
"I'm in over my head."

Behaviors:
Endless hours at work
Isolation from friends
No exercise

John's anxiety and depression led to his behaviors (isolating himself, no exercise, etc.), which in turn worsened his symptoms. Similarly, his thoughts and symptoms reinforced one another, as did his thoughts and behaviors.

We started with behavioral activation: finding activities to address the lack of reward he was getting from life, the social isolation, and the worsening depression.

We then spent several sessions examining his thoughts—how they were not only unhelpful, but also often untrue. For example, he compared himself unfavorably to his dad, a successful self-employed electrician who never seemed as stressed out as John felt. John came to realize that his dad had far fewer financial commitments and worked in a time when the cost of living was much lower. John also realized that his dad probably felt more stress than John realized as a kid, as John's kids probably weren't aware of his own.

Later sessions focused on time and task management, working to help John invest his time productively so he could spend as much time as possible doing what he cared about, especially being with his family and friends. Finally, John practiced facing the fears he had, especially related to something going very wrong at work and his family facing financial ruin.

"I think the biggest factor was getting back to the things I love doing," John said. "It feels like I could've changed my thinking and gotten more efficient at work, but if I'm not enjoying my life, it's kind of like, 'What's the point?'"

John found that adjusting his thinking removed an obstacle to activities he enjoyed. "I used to tell myself, 'You'll regret it if you're not available when something goes wrong at work.' But I realized I couldn't live my whole life waiting for someone's pipes to explode. The only real regret would be if I didn't enjoy my time on Earth."

As you think back to when you started this program and the work you've done since then, let's return to the CBT model and see how the pieces fit together.

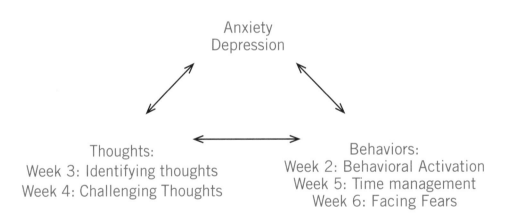

Anxiety
Depression

Thoughts:
Week 3: Identifying thoughts
Week 4: Challenging Thoughts

Behaviors:
Week 2: Behavioral Activation
Week 5: Time management
Week 6: Facing Fears

Think about your experience with each part of the program. Then, consider where you found the most benefit. Which parts do you feel went well? Write your reflections below.

_____

_____

_____

_____

_____

_____

I asked John what changed over the past few weeks. He told me a story. "Last week I was in my office at home, and my four-year-old daughter came in. She was looking for tape or something and didn't realize I was in there. When she saw me, I saw some fear come into her eyes and she started to back out of the room. She'd gotten so used to me being tense and irritable when I was working, so I must've surprised her when I smiled.

"When I did, she actually ran to me and gave me a hug. I scooped her up and we talked for a few minutes, and I felt like I was actually seeing her and hearing her for the first time in as long as I could remember, without a haze of dread and worry clouding everything. Then she hopped down, said, 'Bye, Daddy,' and went back to playing."

John's voice wavered, and his eyes filled with tears. "I couldn't help crying afterward. I was just thinking, 'What's more important than being able to show love to my kids?' I felt such a lightness, where I'd felt a weight before. Now I don't take everything so seriously, and I actually think I'm better at what I do."

Think back over the past six weeks. Does any event stand out that makes you feel like you're moving in the right direction? It could be something that happened at work or with your family or friends. It could be a major development or something subtle. Write about the event below. What do you feel as you think about this event?

_____

_____

_____

_____

_____

_____

As we continued discussing what had worked well for John, I pointed out that the improvements he was seeing didn't just happen—they came from changes he made in his thoughts and actions. With that idea in mind, I asked John what specific things he had done to feel better. Together, we came up with the following list:

- *Spending more time with friends*
- *Trusting my employees and loosening the reins at work (difficult)*
- *Getting regular exercise*
- *Focusing on my family when I'm with them*
- *Minding my thinking*

Different people find different parts of a CBT program more helpful, depending on what they're struggling with and what they need. As you think about the positive changes you've made, what specific things were most helpful?

_____

_____

_____

_____

_____

_____

John also noted areas where he continued to struggle. It was hard not to fall back into worries when a situation came up at work. He also found it easy to skip workouts. While John wasn't exactly where he wanted to be in every way, he felt confident he could use his new tools to continue moving toward his goals.

No matter how much work we put into a CBT program, none of us meets our goals perfectly or feels like "the work is done." In what areas do you want to continue making changes?

_____

_____

_____

_____

_____

Which of the tools from the past six weeks might be helpful in these areas?

_____

_____

_____

_____

Looking Ahead

"Even after all the work I've done over the past few months, I still get waves of anxiety and worry," John said. "But they feel more manageable. It's almost like I feel less anxious because I know I have a way of managing the anxiety."

Based on what he'd found helpful, John and I put together a plan for continuing the progress he'd made. He identified five main factors that led to his feeling better and organized them into a wellness plan. He chose to arrange the five factors into a pentagon, so his plan looked like this:

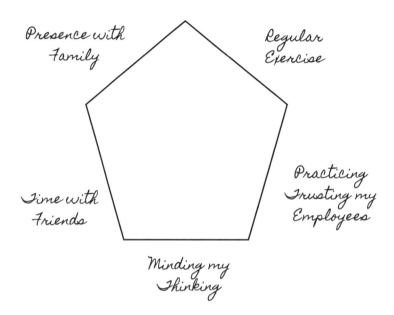

Under each of John's intentions, he listed reminders for himself. For example, under "Presence with family" he included:

- *No constant checking of cell phone*
- *Focus on person I'm talking to*
- *Redirect thoughts when they wander unnecessarily to work*
- *Take care of work issues so they don't intrude*

John kept a copy of this plan with him to refer to, especially when he found himself struggling.

SUMMARIZING WHAT WORKS FOR YOU

All of us need reminders of the things we intend to do. Consider again the most helpful changes you made. What will you need to keep in mind to continue feeling well, and to address any challenges that might arise in the future? Use the space below to summarize your own plan (if you need more space, use the Notes section at the end of the book). Feel free to be creative in the way you organize your ideas. What's important is that it resonates with you.

_____

_____

_____

_____

I'm often struck by how easy it is to let slip the activities that keep us feeling well. For example, if I'm not careful, I can easily let exercise fall by the wayside. Changes in our lives can also affect our well-being in ways we might not recognize at first, like when friends move away and we lose an important source of support.

When we find our mood dropping or anxiety rising, we can consult the plan we laid out for ourselves. By running through the various factors, we can identify ones we need to focus on to feel our best again. Plan to return to your own summary at least weekly, and whenever you need reminders about what helps you feel well.

MEETING FUTURE CHALLENGES

Toward the end of our session, I asked John an important question: What could happen that might lead to a major setback, if he isn't careful? He answered immediately: "If one of my best guys decides to move on. The last time that happened, I was a wreck for weeks. I had to pick up the slack while I found someone to take his place, which created strain at home. And the whole process of trying to find someone I can trust really pushes my buttons. Just thinking about it now makes me feel anxious. What if I can't find someone, or I pick someone who's no good? There are so many unknowns."

I asked John what tools he has now that he might not have had before. "Well, I know now I can deal with my anxiety, which is a total game changer. And I can remind myself to accept the uncertainty, and focus on what I can control. Because in the end, I know it's going to be okay." He brightened a little. "I actually think it'd be a great test of what I've learned."

Just as John did, think about any life event that could set you back. Are there events that are possible—or even inevitable—that you'll need to prepare for? What tools will help you face these challenges?

_____

_____

_____

_____

_____

_____

_____

_____

_____

_____

MINDFULNESS

One of the most helpful tools for staying well is to practice focusing our attention on the present and being open to our experience just as it is. In fact, this approach is embedded throughout this book—for example, in the practice of learning to tolerate uncertainty and accept ourselves, struggles and all. Even recognizing my thoughts *as thoughts*—not as absolute truth—is part of this practice.

The concept of mindfulness describes this present-focused, nonjudgmental approach to living. A 2011 *Clinical Psychology Review* article concluded that training in mindfulness is a powerful protector against relapse following CBT for people with recurrent depression.

For example, a 2004 study by Ma and Teasdale found relapse rates were cut by more than 50 percent among individuals who received mindfulness-based CBT compared to those who got other kinds of therapy. While an exhaustive discussion of mindfulness is beyond the scope of this book, you might consider whether mindfulness could be helpful to you. I've included some resources on mindfulness at the end of the book (page 204) to get you started.

ADDITIONAL GOALS

After several weeks in treatment, John realized there were other life areas he wanted to work on that he hadn't thought of before. For example, he'd felt a certain distance from his wife that he wanted to talk with her about in the near future. He also saw that his sleep had been bad for so long he'd stopped noticing. He decided to discuss these issues in treatment and address them with the CBT tools at his disposal.

Oftentimes, after we've learned CBT techniques, we'll start to see other areas of our lives where we could apply them. Clearing away the worst of our anxiety and depression can make room for other things to work on. For example, we might decide to address issues related to our careers, spirituality, relationships, substance use, sleep, or anything else.

Have other goals come to mind since you started this program? If so, write them below. If not, simply continue focusing on your pretreatment goals.

_____

_____

_____

_____

_____

_____

_____

_____

Saying Goodbye

It feels strange to say goodbye to someone I've never met (most likely), and yet I don't want to end without saying it. We've traveled the pages of this book together: I in the writing, you in the doing. As we part ways, I want to thank you for the opportunity to work with you. My hope is that your depression and/or anxiety feel more manageable, and that you feel more connected to your strengths, your loved ones, and your experience.

I would also encourage you to expect to still have some struggles. No book and no amount of work will get rid of all anxiety, or the ups and downs of being alive. In this context, I often think of a quote from a book by Hermann Hesse called *Narcissus and Goldmund*; one of the characters says that there is no peace "that lives within us constantly and never leaves us. There is only the peace that must be won again and again, each new day of our lives."

By finding what works for you and learning to be, in a way, your own therapist, you can find that peace as often as you need to.

You've reached the end of this seven-week CBT program. You have no doubt done a great deal of work toward your goals. I hope you're feeling good about the work you've done and the progress you've made. Changing our thoughts and behaviors is hard work.

Take a few moments to check in with how you're doing. What do you feel as you reflect on the past few weeks? What are your thoughts as you look to the weeks and months ahead?

_____

_____

_____

_____

_____

_____

_____

_____

_____

_____

_____

_____

_____

_____

_____

ACTIVITY PLAN

1 Keep working up your fear hierarchy if you're practicing facing your fears.
2 Continue to practice the other techniques you found helpful.
3 Return to the relevant chapters as needed.
4 Consult the Resources section at the back of this book for additional tools.

The Next Seven Weeks

Using What You've Learned, and What to Do If You're Still Struggling

Several years ago as I was doing physical therapy for a sports-related injury, I was struck by the many parallels between PT and CBT. Like CBT, PT is hard work, and requires moving through discomfort to reach a better place. PT also provides a structured plan like CBT does for regaining health and function, and the work between sessions is equally important in therapy for the body and therapy for the mind.

The two therapies are also similar in that the issues that brought us to treatment are rarely resolved completely during the course of therapy. Instead, we look for *progress* to tell us the exercises we're doing are working. If we're moving in the right direction, we're probably practicing the right exercises. After the course of PT is over we avoid re-injury by continuing a key set of exercises that will keep us well.

Now that you've finished this program, the next seven weeks are a crucial time for you to keep moving in a positive direction. If you've made significant progress during the program you may be able to cut back on some of the more focused CBT work as you move into a maintenance phase. For example, you may not need to be as strict with scheduling activities or monitoring thoughts.

At the same time, beware of subtle ways of losing the ground you've gained. Be especially careful to prevent avoidance, which is powerfully addictive. And while I don't want a person to feel like progress is fragile, it's important to be vigilant for signs of slipping backward so you can employ the tools you have when needed. When in doubt over the next seven weeks (and beyond), err on the side of adhering to the practices that got you better. Remember to refer to your personal plan that summarizes what to do to feel well.

When to Consult a Professional

If you don't feel like this program has helped you—either because it didn't seem to address your struggles or you weren't able to really engage with the program—it may be a good idea to seek professional help. While many people are able to benefit from using a book like this one without a therapist's guidance, others require a higher level of care.

The Resources section in the back of this book has websites through which you can find the CBT therapists nearest you. You can also ask your primary care doctor for a recommendation. It's essential that you feel like you have a good working relationship with a therapist, so aim to find a therapist who is a good match for you.

Wherever you find yourself at the end of this program, I encourage you to continue pushing ahead toward the life you want. I wish you the very best in the journey.

Resources

Online Resources

Try the following online resources for greater learning, for finding professional help, and for diving deeper into treatments and techniques.

ANXIETY AND DEPRESSION

Anxiety and Depression Association of America (ADAA)
http://www.adaa.org/understanding-anxiety
The ADAA website discusses what distinguishes normal anxiety and depression from a disorder, provides statistics about these conditions, and has information about obsessive-compulsive disorder (OCD) and posttraumatic stress disorder (PTSD).

National Institute of Mental Health (NIMH)
Anxiety: www.nimh.nih.gov/health/topics/anxiety-disorders/index.shtml
Depression: www.nimh.nih.gov/health/topics/depression/index.shtml
These websites describe common symptoms of depression and anxiety, discuss risk factors and treatments, and include how to find clinical trials you might qualify for. They also include links to free booklets and brochures.

FINDING HELP

Association for Behavioral and Cognitive Therapies (ABCT)
Find a CBT Therapist: www.findcbt.org
This website allows you to search for CBT therapists by ZIP code, specialty, and accepted insurance.

Psychological Treatments:
www.abct.org/Information/?m=mInformation&fa=_psychoTreatments
This website from the leading professional organization for CBT therapists covers topics like evidence-based practice, treatment options, and choosing a therapist.

Society of Clinical Psychology (SCP)
Research-Supported Treatments: http://www.div12.org/psychological-treatments/
Division 12 of the American Psychological Association, the Society of Clinical Psychology (SCP), maintains a list of research-supported psychological treatments. The website is searchable by treatment and psychological condition.

SUPPORT GROUPS

Anxiety and Depression Association of America (ADAA)
http://www.adaa.org/supportgroups
The ADAA provides information about support groups by state (as well as some international listings), including contact information for the support groups.

National Alliance on Mental Illness (NAMI)
www.nami.org/Find-Support
The NAMI website offers ways to find support whether you or a loved one has a psychological disorder. Many additional resources are available on the site, including links to local NAMI chapters.

MINDFULNESS

Mindfulnet.org
www.mindfulnet.org/index.htm
This website is a clearinghouse of information about mindfulness: what it is, how it's used, research that supports it, and more.

Books

Many of these books are on the Association for Behavioral and Cognitive Therapy's Books of Merit list, meaning they describe a treatment that was based on solid research evidence. The full list can be found at **www.abct.org/SHBooks**.

DEPRESSION AND ANXIETY

Davis, Martha, Elizabeth Robbins Eshelman, and Matthew McKay. *The Relaxation and Stress Reduction Workbook*, 6th edition.

Ellis, Albert, and Robert A. Harper. *A New Guide to Rational Living.*

Otto, Michael, and Jasper Smits. *Exercise for Mood and Anxiety: Proven Strategies for Overcoming Depression and Enhancing Well-Being.*

DEPRESSION

Addis, Michael E., and Christopher R. Martell. *Overcoming Depression One Step at a Time: The New Behavioral Activation Approach to Getting Your Life Back.*

Burns, David D. *The Feeling Good Handbook*, Revised edition.

Greenberger, Dennis, and Christine A. Padesky. *Mind Over Mood: Change How You Feel by Changing the Way You Think*, 2nd edition.

Joiner, Thomas Jr., and Jeremy Pettit. *The Interpersonal Solution to Depression: A Workbook for Changing How You Feel by Changing How You Relate.*

ANXIETY

Antony, Martin M., and Peter J. Norton. *The Anti-Anxiety Workbook.*

Antony, Martin M., and Richard P. Swinson. *The Shyness and Social Anxiety Workbook: Proven Techniques for Overcoming Your Fears.*

Carbonell, David. *Panic Attacks Workbook: A Guided Program for Beating the Panic Trick.*

Clark, David A., and Aaron T. Beck. *The Anxiety and Worry Workbook: The Cognitive Behavioral Solution.*

Cooper, Hattie C. *Thriving with Social Anxiety: Daily Strategies for Overcoming Anxiety and Building Self-Confidence.*

Hope, Debra A., Richard G. Heimberg, and Cynthia L. Turk. *Managing Social Anxiety: A Cognitive-Behavioral Therapy Approach: Workbook*, 2nd edition.

Leahy, Robert L. *The Worry Cure: Seven Steps to Stop Worry from Stopping You.*

Reinecke, Mark. *Little Ways to Keep Calm and Carry On: Twenty Lessons for Managing Worry, Anxiety, and Fear.*

Robichaud, Melisa, and Michel J. Dugas. *The Generalized Anxiety Disorder Workbook: A Comprehensive CBT Guide for Coping with Uncertainty, Worry, and Fear.*

Tolin, David. *Face Your Fears: A Proven Plan to Beat Anxiety, Panic, Phobias, and Obsessions.*

Tompkins, Michael A. *Anxiety and Avoidance: A Universal Treatment for Anxiety, Panic, and Fear.*

White, Elke Zuercher. *An End to Panic: Breakthrough Techniques for Overcoming Panic Disorder.*

MINDFULNESS

Germer, Christopher K. *The Mindful Path to Self-Compassion: Freeing Yourself from Destructive Thoughts and Emotions.*

Kabat-Zinn, Jon. *Full Catastrophe Living: Using the Wisdom of Your Body and Mind to Face Stress, Pain, and Illness*, Revised ed.

Orsillo, Susan M., and Lizabeth Roemer. *The Mindful Way through Anxiety: Break Free from Chronic Worry and Reclaim Your Life.*

Teasdale, John D., and Zindel V. Segal. *The Mindful Way Through Depression: Freeing Yourself from Chronic Unhappiness.*

References

Abramson, Lyn Y., Gerald I. Metalsky, and Lauren B. Alloy. "Hopelessness Depression: A Theory-Based Subtype of Depression." *Psychological Review* 96, no. 2 (April 1989): 358–372. doi:10.1037/0033-295X.96.2.358.

American Psychiatric Association. *Diagnostic and Statistical Manual of Mental Disorders, 5th ed. (DSM-5)*. Arlington, VA: American Psychiatric Publishing, 2013.

Antony, Martin M. "Behavior Therapy." In *Current Psychotherapies*, 10th ed., edited by Danny Wedding and Raymond J. Corsini, 193–230. Salt Lake City, UT: Brooks/Cole Publishing, 2013.

Asmundson, Gordon J. G., Mathew G. Fetzner, Lindsey B. DeBoer, Mark B. Powers, Michael W. Otto, and Jasper AJ Smits. "Let's Get Physical: A Contemporary Review of the Anxiolytic Effects of Exercise for Anxiety and Its Disorders." *Depression and Anxiety* 30, no. 4 (April 2013): 362–373. doi:10.1002/da.22043.

Association for Behavioral and Cognitive Therapies. "ABCT Fact Sheets: Guidelines for Choosing a Therapist." Accessed June 20, 2016. http://www.abct.org/Information/?m=mInformation&fa=fs_GUIDELINES_CHOOSING.

Association for Behavioral and Cognitive Therapies. "How It All Began." Accessed June 20, 2016. http://www.abct.org/About/?m=mAbout&fa=History.

Barth, Jürgen, Martina Schumacher, and Christoph Herrmann-Lingen. "Depression as a Risk Factor for Mortality in Patients with Coronary Heart Disease: A Meta-Analysis." *Psychosomatic Medicine* 66, no. 6 (November/December 2004): 802–813. doi:10.1097/01.psy.0000146332.53619.b2.

Be, Daniel, Mark A. Whisman, and Lisa A. Uebelacker. "Prospective Associations Between Marital Adjustment and Life Satisfaction." *Personal Relationships* 20, no. 4 (December 2013): 728–739. doi:10.1111/pere.12011.

Beck, Aaron T. "Thinking and Depression: I. Idiosyncratic Content and Cognitive Distortions." *Archives of General Psychiatry* 9, no. 4 (October 1963): 324–333. doi:10.1001/archpsyc.1963.01720160014002.

Beck, Aaron T. "Cognitive Therapy: Nature and Relation to Behavior Therapy." *Behavior Therapy* 1, no. 2 (May 1970): 184–200. doi:10.1016/S0005-7894(70)80030-2.

Beck, Aaron T., A. John Rush, Brian F. Shaw, and Gary Emery. *Cognitive Therapy of Depression*. New York: Guilford Press, 1979.

Beck, Aaron T. *Cognitive Therapy and the Emotional Disorders*. New York: Penguin Books, 1979.

Beck, Aaron T. "The Evolution of the Cognitive Model of Depression and Its Neurobiological Correlates." *American Journal of Psychiatry* 165, no. 8 (August 2008): 969–977. doi:10.1176/appi.ajp.2008.08050721.

Beck, Aaron T., and David JA Dozois. "Cognitive Therapy: Current Status and Future Directions." *Annual Review of Medicine* 62 (2011): 397–409. doi:10.1146/annurev-med-052209-100032.

Beck, Judith S. *Cognitive Behavior Therapy: Basics and Beyond*, 2nd ed. New York: Guilford Press, 2011.

Borkovec, Thomas D., Oscar M. Alcaine, and Evelyn Behar. "Avoidance Theory of Worry and Generalized Anxiety Disorder." In *Generalized Anxiety Disorder: Advances in Research and Practice*, edited by Richard G. Heimberg, Cynthia L. Turk, and Douglas S. Mennin, 77–108. New York: Guilford Press, 2004.

Butler, Andrew C., Jason E. Chapman, Evan M. Forman, and Aaron T. Beck. "The Empirical Status of Cognitive-Behavioral Therapy: A Review of Meta-Analyses." *Clinical Psychology Review* 26, no. 1 (January 2006): 17–31. doi:10.1016/j.cpr.2005.07.003.

Chu, Brian C., Daniela Colognori, Adam S. Weissman, and Katie Bannon. "An Initial Description and Pilot of Group Behavioral Activation Therapy for Anxious and Depressed Youth." *Cognitive and Behavioral Practice* 16, no. 4 (November 2009): 408–419. doi:10.1016/j.cbpra.2009.04.003.

Cole-King, A, and K. G. Harding. "Psychological Factors and Delayed Healing in Chronic Wounds." *Psychosomatic Medicine* 63, no. 2 (March–April 2001): 216–220. doi:10.1.1.570.3740.

Cooney, Gary M., Kerry Dwan, Carolyn A. Greig, Debbie A. Lawlor, Jane Rimer, Fiona R. Waugh, Marion McMurdo, and Gillian E. Mead. "Exercise for Depression." *Cochrane Database of Systematic Reviews*, Issue 9 (2013). Art. No.: CD004366. doi:10.1002/14651858.CD004366.pub6.

Cooper, Andrew A., Alexander C. Kline, Belinda P. M. Graham, Michele Bedard-Gilligan, Patricia G. Mello, Norah C. Feeny, and Lori A. Zoellner. "Homework 'Dose,' Type, and Helpfulness as Predictors of Clinical Outcomes in Prolonged Exposure for PTSD." *Behavior Therapy* (2016). doi:10.1016/j.beth.2016.02.013.

Craske, Michelle G., and David H. Barlow. *Mastery of Your Anxiety and Panic: Workbook*, 4th ed. New York: Oxford University Press, 2006.

Craske, Michelle G., Katharina Kircanski, Moriel Zelikowsky, Jayson Mystkowski, Najwa Chowdhury, and Aaron Baker. "Optimizing Inhibitory Learning During Exposure Therapy." *Behaviour Research and Therapy* 46, no. 1 (January 2008): 5–27. doi:10.1016/j.brat.2007.10.003.

Cuijpers, Pieter. "Bibliotherapy in Unipolar Depression: A Meta-Analysis." *Journal of Behavior Therapy and Experimental Psychiatry* 28, no. 2 (June 1997): 139–147. doi:10.1016/S0005-7916(97)00005-0.

Cuijpers, Pim, Tara Donker, Annemieke van Straten, J. Li, and Gerhard Andersson. "Is Guided Self-Help as Effective as Face-to-Face Psychotherapy for Depression and Anxiety Disorders? A Systematic Review and Meta-Analysis of Comparative Outcome Studies." *Psychological Medicine* 40, no. 12 (December 2010): 1943–1957. doi:10.1017/S0033291710000772.

Dimidjian, Sona, Steven D. Hollon, Keith S. Dobson, Karen B. Schmaling, Robert J. Kohlenberg, Michael E. Addis, Robert Gallop et al. "Randomized Trial of Behavioral Activation, Cognitive Therapy, and Antidepressant Medication in the Acute Treatment of Adults With Major Depression." *Journal of Consulting and Clinical Psychology* 74, no. 4 (August 2006): 658–670. doi:10.1037/0022-006X.74.4.658.

Division 12 of the American Psychological Association. "Research-Supported Psychological Treatments." Accessed June 20, 2016. https://www.div12.org/psychological -treatments.

Doering, Lynn V., Debra K. Moser, Walter Lemankiewicz, Cristina Luper, and Steven Khan. "Depression, Healing and Recovery From Coronary Artery Bypass Surgery." *American Journal of Critical Care* 14, no. 4 (July 2005): 316–324. doi:10.1.1.607.8304.

Dugas, Michel J., Pascale Brillon, Pierre Savard, Julie Turcotte, Adrienne Gaudet, Robert Ladouceur, Renée Leblanc, and Nicole J. Gervais. "A Randomized Clinical Trial of Cognitive-Behavioral Therapy and Applied Relaxation for Adults with Generalized Anxiety Disorder." *Behavior Therapy* 41, no. 1 (March 2010): 46–58. doi:10.1016/ j.beth.2008.12.004.

The Economist. "Air Safety: A Crash Course in Probability." Accessed June 21, 2016. http://www.economist.com/blogs/gulliver/2015/01/air-safety.

Egan, Gerard. *The Skilled Helper*, 6th ed. Pacific Grove, CA: Brooks/Cole, 1998.

Ellis, Albert. *Reason and Emotion in Psychotherapy*. Secaucus, NJ: Citadel Press, 1962.

Ellis, Albert. *Overcoming Destructive Beliefs, Feelings, and Behaviors: New Directions for Rational Emotive Behavior Therapy*. Amherst, NY: Prometheus Books, 2001.

Ellis, Albert, and Catherine MacLaren. *Rational Emotive Behavior Therapy: A Therapist's Guide*, 2nd ed. Atascadero, CA: Impact Publishers, 2005.

Epictetus. *Enchiridion*. Mineola, NY: Dover Publications, 2004.

Epperson, C. Neill, Meir Steiner, S. Ann Hartlage, Elias Eriksson, Peter J. Schmidt, Ian Jones, and Kimberly A. Yonkers. "Premenstrual Dysphoric Disorder: Evidence for a New Category for *DSM-5*." *American Journal of Psychiatry* (May 2012): 465–475. doi:10.1176/appi.ajp.2012.11081302.

Eysenck, Hans Jurgen. *Behaviour Therapy and the Neuroses.* Oxford: Pergamon, 1960.

Fernie, Bruce A., Marcantonio M. Spada, Ana V. Nikčević, George A. Georgiou, and Giovanni B. Moneta. "Metacognitive Beliefs About Procrastination: Development and Concurrent Validity of a Self-Report Questionnaire." *Journal of Cognitive Psychotherapy* 23, no. 4 (2009): 283–293. doi:10.1891/0889-8391.23.4.283.

Foa, Edna B., and Michael J. Kozak. "Emotional Processing of Fear: Exposure to Corrective Information." *Psychological Bulletin* 99, no. 1 (January 1986): 20–35. doi:10.1037/0033-2909.99.1.20.

Francis, Kylie, and Michel J. Dugas. "Assessing Positive Beliefs About Worry: Validation of a Structured Interview." *Personality and Individual Differences* 37, no. 2 (July 2004): 405–415. doi:10.1016/j.paid.2003.09.012.

Freud, Sigmund. *An Outline of Psycho-Analysis.* New York: W. W. Norton and Company, 1949.

Gawrysiak, Michael, Christopher Nicholas, and Derek R. Hopko. "Behavioral Activation for Moderately Depressed University Students: Randomized Controlled Trial." *Journal of Counseling Psychology* 56, no. 3 (July 2009): 468–475. doi:10.1037/a0016383.

Gellatly, Judith, Peter Bower, Sue Hennessy, David Richards, Simon Gilbody, and Karina Lovell. "What Makes Self-Help Interventions Effective in the Management of Depressive Symptoms? Meta-Analysis and Meta-Regression." *Psychological Medicine* 37, no. 9 (September 2007): 1217–1228. doi:10.1017/S0033291707000062.

Gillihan, Seth J., E. A. Hembree, and E. B. Foa. "Behavior Therapy: Exposure Therapy for Anxiety Disorders." In *The Art and Science of Brief Psychotherapies: An Illustrated Guide*, edited by Mantosh J. Dewan, Brett N. Steenbarger, and Roger P. Greenberg, 83–120. Arlington, VA: American Psychiatric Publishing, 2012.

Gillihan, Seth J., and Edna B. Foa. "Exposure-Based Interventions for Adult Anxiety Disorders, Obsessive-Compulsive Disorder, and Posttraumatic Stress Disorder." In *The Oxford Handbook of Cognitive and Behavioral Therapies*, edited by Christine Maguth Nezu and Arthur M. Nezu, 96–117. New York: Oxford University Press, 2015.

Gillihan, Seth J., Monnica T. Williams, Emily Malcoun, Elna Yadin, and Edna B. Foa. "Common Pitfalls in Exposure and Response Prevention (EX/RP) for OCD." *Journal of Obsessive-Compulsive and Related Disorders* 1, no. 4 (October 2012): 251–257. doi:10.1016/j.jocrd.2012.05.002.

Goldfried, Marvin R., and Gerald C. Davison. *Clinical Behavior Therapy*. New York: John Wiley and Sons, 1994.

Haaga, David A., Murray J. Dyck, and Donald Ernst. "Empirical Status of Cognitive Theory of Depression." *Psychological Bulletin* 110, no. 2 (September 1991): 215–236. doi:10.1037/0033-2909.110.2.215.

Hallion, Lauren S., and Ayelet Meron Ruscio. "A Meta-Analysis of the Effect of Cognitive Bias Modification on Anxiety and Depression." *Psychological Bulletin* 137, no. 6 (November 2011): 940–958. doi:10.1037/a0024355.

Hellström, Kerstin, and Lars-Göran Öst. "One-Session Therapist Directed Exposure vs Two Forms of Manual Directed Self-Exposure in the Treatment of Spider Phobia." *Behaviour Research and Therapy* 33, no. 8 (November 1995): 959–965. doi:10.1016/0005-7967(95)00028-V.

Hesse, Hermann. *Narcissus and Goldmund*. Translated by Ursule Molinaro. New York: Farrar, Straus and Giroux, 1968.

Hirai, Michiyo, and George A. Clum. "A Meta-Analytic Study of Self-Help Interventions for Anxiety Problems." *Behavior Therapy* 37, no. 2 (June 2006): 99–111. doi:10.1016/j.beth.2005.05.002.

Hofmann, Stefan G., Anu Asnaani, Imke JJ Vonk, Alice T. Sawyer, and Angela Fang. "The Efficacy of Cognitive Behavioral Therapy: A Review of Meta-Analyses." *Cognitive Therapy and Research* 36, no. 5 (October 2012): 427–440. doi:10.1007/s10608-012-9476-1.

Hollon, Steven D., Robert J. DeRubeis, Richard C. Shelton, Jay D. Amsterdam, Ronald M. Salomon, John P. O'Reardon, Margaret L. Lovett et al. "Prevention of Relapse Following Cognitive Therapy vs Medications in Moderate to Severe Depression." *Archives of General Psychiatry* 62, no. 4 (April 2005): 417–422. doi:10.1001/archpsyc.62.4.417.

Homer. *The Odyssey, Book XII*, translated by Samuel Butler. Accessed June 23, 2016. http://classics.mit.edu/Homer/odyssey.12.xii.html.

Hopko, Derek R., C. W. Lejuez, and Sandra D. Hopko. "Behavioral Activation as an Intervention for Coexistent Depressive and Anxiety Symptoms." *Clinical Case Studies* 3, no. 1 (January 2004): 37–48. doi:10.1177/1534650103258969.

Kaufman, Joan, Bao-Zhu Yang, Heather Douglas-Palumberi, Shadi Houshyar, Deborah Lipschitz, John H. Krystal, and Joel Gelernter. "Social Supports and Serotonin Transporter Gene Moderate Depression in Maltreated Children." *Proceedings of the National Academy of Sciences of the United States of America* 101, no. 49 (December 2004): 17,316–17,321. doi:10.1073/pnas.0404376101.

Kazantzis, Nikolaos, Craig Whittington, and Frank Dattilio. "Meta Analysis of Homework Effects in Cognitive and Behavioral Therapy: A Replication and Extension." *Clinical Psychology: Science and Practice* 17, no. 2 (June 2010): 144–156. doi:10.1111/j.1468-2850.2010.01204.x.

Kazdin, Alan E. "Evaluation of the Automatic Thoughts Questionnaire: Negative Cognitive Processes and Depression Among Children." *Psychological Assessment: A Journal of Consulting and Clinical Psychology* 2, no. 1 (March 1990): 73–79. doi:10.1037/1040-3590.2.1.73.

Keeley, Mary L., Eric A. Storch, Lisa J. Merlo, and Gary R. Geffken. "Clinical Predictors of Response to Cognitive-Behavioral Therapy for Obsessive-Compulsive Disorder." *Clinical Psychology Review* 28, no. 1 (January 2008): 118–130. doi:10.1016/j.cpr.2007.04.003.

Kessler, Ronald C., Patricia Berglund, Olga Demler, Robert Jin, Doreen Koretz, Kathleen R. Merikangas, A. John Rush, Ellen E. Walters, and Philip S. Wang. "The Epidemiology of Major Depressive Disorder: Results from the National Comorbidity Survey Replication (NCS-R)." *Journal of the American Medical Association* 289, no. 23 (June 2003): 3095–3105. doi:10.1001/jama.289.23.3095.

Kessler, Ronald C., Patricia Berglund, Olga Demler, Robert Jin, Kathleen R. Merikangas, and Ellen E. Walters. "Lifetime Prevalence and Age-of-Onset Distributions of *DSM-IV* Disorders in the National Comorbidity Survey Replication." *Archives of General Psychiatry* 62, no. 6 (June 2005): 593–602. doi:10.1001/archpsyc.62.6.593.

Kessler, Ronald C., Wai Tat Chiu, Olga Demler, and Ellen E. Walters. "Prevalence, Severity, and Comorbidity of 12-month *DSM-IV* Disorders in the National Comorbidity Survey Replication." *Archives of General Psychiatry* 62, no. 6 (June 2005): 617–627. doi:10.1001/archpsyc.62.6.617.

Kessler, Ronald C., Wai Tat Chiu, Robert Jin, Ayelet Meron Ruscio, Katherine Shear, and Ellen E. Walters. "The Epidemiology of Panic Attacks, Panic Disorder, and Agoraphobia in the National Comorbidity Survey Replication." *Archives of General Psychiatry* 63, no. 4 (April 2006): 415–424. doi:10.1001/archpsyc.63.4.415.

Kessler, Ronald C., Maria Petukhova, Nancy A. Sampson, Alan M. Zaslavsky, and Hans Ullrich Wittchen. "Twelve Month and Lifetime Prevalence and Lifetime Morbid Risk of Anxiety and Mood Disorders in the United States." *International Journal of Methods in Psychiatric Research* 21, no. 3 (September 2012): 169–184. doi:10.1002/mpr.1359.

Kessler, Ronald C., Ayelet Meron Ruscio, Katherine Shear, and Hans-Ulrich Wittchen. "Epidemiology of Anxiety Disorders." *Behavioral Neurobiology of Anxiety and Its Treatment*, edited by Murray B. Stein and Thomas Steckler, 21–35. Heidelberg, Germany: Springer, 2009.

Kroenke, Kurt, Robert L. Spitzer, and Janet B. W. Williams. "The PHQ 9." *Journal of General Internal Medicine* 16, no. 9 (September 2001): 606–613. doi:10.1046/j.1525-1497.2001.016009606.x.

Krogh, Jesper, Merete Nordentoft, Jonathan A. C. Sterne, and Debbie A. Lawlor. "The Effect of Exercise in Clinically Depressed Adults: Systematic Review and Meta-Analysis of Randomized Controlled Trials." *The Journal of Clinical Psychiatry* 72, no. 4 (2011): 529–538. doi:10.4088/JCP.08r04913blu.

Ladouceur, Robert, Patrick Gosselin, and Michel J. Dugas. "Experimental Manipulation of Intolerance of Uncertainty: A Study of a Theoretical Model of Worry." *Behaviour Research and Therapy* 38, no. 9 (September 2000): 933–941. doi:10.1016/S0005-7967(99)00133-3.

Lazarus, Arnold A. *Multimodal Behavior Therapy*. New York: Springer Publishing Company, 1976.

Leary, Mark R., and Sarah Meadows. "Predictors, Elicitors, and Concomitants of Social Blushing." *Journal of Personality and Social Psychology* 60, no. 2 (February 1991): 254–262. doi:10.1037/0022-3514.60.2.254.

Lejuez, C. W., Derek R. Hopko, Ron Acierno, Stacey B. Daughters, and Sherry L. Pagoto. "Ten Year Revision of the Brief Behavioral Activation Treatment for Depression: Revised Treatment Manual." *Behavior Modification* 35, no. 2 (March 2011): 111–161. doi:10.1177/0145445510390929.

Liu, Xinghua, Sisi Wang, Shaochen Chang, Wenjun Chen, and Mei Si. "Effect of Brief Mindfulness Intervention on Tolerance and Distress of Pain Induced by Cold-Pressor Task." *Stress and Health* 29, no. 3 (August 2013): 199–204. doi:10.1002/smi.2446.

Löwe, Bernd, Kurt Kroenke, Wolfgang Herzog, and Kerstin Gräfe. "Measuring Depression Outcome with a Brief Self-Report Instrument: Sensitivity to Change of the Patient Health Questionnaire (PHQ-9)." *Journal of Affective Disorders* 81, no. 1 (July 2004): 61–66. doi:10.1016/S0165-0327(03)00198-8.

Ma, S. Helen, and John D. Teasdale. "Mindfulness-Based Cognitive Therapy for Depression: Replication and Exploration of Differential Relapse Prevention Effects." *Journal of Consulting and Clinical Psychology* 72, no. 1 (February 2004): 31–40. doi:10.1037/0022-006X.72.1.31.

Martin, Alexandra, Winfried Rief, Antje Klaiberg, and Elmar Braehler. "Validity of the Brief Patient Health Questionnaire Mood Scale (PHQ-9) in the General Population." *General Hospital Psychiatry* 28, no. 1 (January–February 2006): 71–77. doi:10.1016/j.genhosppsych.2005.07.003.

McClatchy, Steve. *Decide.* Hoboken, NJ: Wiley, 2014.

McLean, Carmen P., Anu Asnaani, Brett T. Litz, and Stefan G. Hofmann. "Gender Differences in Anxiety Disorders: Prevalence, Course of Illness, Comorbidity and Burden of Illness." *Journal of Psychiatric Research* 45, no. 8 (August 2011): 1027–1035. doi:10.1016/j.jpsychires.2011.03.006.

McManus, Freda, David M. Clark, and Ann Hackmann. "Specificity of Cognitive Biases in Social Phobia and Their Role in Recovery." *Behavioural and Cognitive Psychotherapy* 28, no. 03 (July 2000): 201–209. doi:10.1017/S1352465800003015.

Medco Health Solutions, Inc., "America's State of Mind Report." Accessed June 21, 2016. http://apps.who.int/medicinedocs/documents/s19032en/s19032en.pdf.

Mitchell, Matthew D., Philip Gehrman, Michael Perlis, and Craig A. Umscheid. "Comparative Effectiveness of Cognitive Behavioral Therapy for Insomnia: A Systematic Review." *BMC Family Practice* 13 (May 2012): 1–11. doi:10.1186/1471-2296-13-40.

Moscovitch, David A. "What Is the Core Fear in Social Phobia? A New Model to Facilitate Individualized Case Conceptualization and Treatment." *Cognitive and Behavioral Practice* 16, no. 2 (May 2009): 123–134. doi:10.1016/j.cbpra.2008.04.002.

Naragon-Gainey, Kristin. "Meta-Analysis of the Relations of Anxiety Sensitivity to the Depressive and Anxiety Disorders." *Psychological Bulletin* 136, no. 1 (January 2010): 128–150. doi:10.1037/a0018055.

Nolen-Hoeksema, Susan, Blair E. Wisco, and Sonja Lyubomirsky. "Rethinking Rumination." *Perspectives on Psychological Science* 3, no. 5 (September 2008): 400–424. doi:10.1111/j.1745-6924.2008.00088.x.

Okajima, Isa, Yoko Komada, and Yuichi Inoue. "A Meta-Analysis on the Treatment Effectiveness of Cognitive Behavioral Therapy for Primary Insomnia." *Sleep and Biological Rhythms* 9, no. 1 (January 2011): 24–34. doi:10.1111/j.1479-8425.2010.00481.x.

Öst, Lars-Göran. "One-Session Treatment for Specific Phobias." *Behaviour Research and Therapy* 27, no. 1 (1989): 1–7. doi:10.1016/0005-7967(89)90113-7.

Pavlov, Ivan P. "The Scientific Investigation of the Psychical Faculties or Processes in the Higher Animals." *Science* 24, no. 620 (November 1906): 613–619. doi:10.1126/science.24.620.613.

Piet, Jacob, and Esben Hougaard. "The Effect of Mindfulness-Based Cognitive Therapy for Prevention of Relapse in Recurrent Major Depressive Disorder: A Systematic Review and Meta-Analysis." *Clinical Psychology Review* 31, no. 6 (August 2011): 1032–1040. doi:10.1016/j.cpr.2011.05.002.

Rachman, Stanley. *The Effects of Psychotherapy*. Oxford: Pergamon Press, 1971.

Redmoon, Ambrose. "No Peaceful Warriors." *Gnosis Journal*, Fall 1991.

Robustelli, Briana L., Anne C. Trytko, Angela Li, and Mark A. Whisman. "Marital Discord and Suicidal Outcomes in a National Sample of Married Individuals." *Suicide and Life-Threatening Behavior* 45, no. 5 (October 2015): 623–632. doi:10.1111/sltb.12157.

Rothbaum, Barbara, Edna B. Foa, and Elizabeth Hembree. *Reclaiming Your Life from a Traumatic Experience: A Prolonged Exposure Treatment Program Workbook*. New York: Oxford University Press, 2007.

Schmidt, Norman B., and Kelly Woolaway-Bickel. "The Effects of Treatment Compliance on Outcome in Cognitive-Behavioral Therapy for Panic Disorder: Quality Versus Quantity." *Journal of Consulting and Clinical Psychology* 68, no. 1 (February 2000): 13–18. doi:10.1037/0022-006X.68.1.13.

Sheldon, Kennon M., and Andrew J. Elliot. "Goal Striving, Need Satisfaction, and Longitudinal Well-Being: The Self-Concordance Model." *Journal of Personality and Social Psychology* 76, no. 3 (March 1999): 482–497. doi:10.1037/0022-3514.76.3.482.

Skinner, Burrhus Frederic. *The Behavior of Organisms: An Experimental Analysis*. Cambridge, MA: B. F. Skinner Foundation, 1991.

Solomon, Laura J., and Esther D. Rothblum. "Academic Procrastination: Frequency and Cognitive-Behavioral Correlates." *Journal of Counseling Psychology* 31, no. 4 (October 1984): 503–509. doi:10.1037/0022-0167.31.4.503.

Spek, Viola, Pim Cuijpers, Ivan Nyklícek, Heleen Riper, Jules Keyzer, and Victor Pop. "Internet-Based Cognitive Behaviour Therapy for Symptoms of Depression and Anxiety: A Meta-Analysis." *Psychological Medicine* 37, no. 3 (March 2007): 319–328. doi:10.1017/S0033291706008944.

Stathopoulou, Georgia, Mark B. Powers, Angela C. Berry, Jasper A. J. Smits, and Michael W. Otto. "Exercise Interventions for Mental Health: A Quantitative and Qualitative Review." *Clinical Psychology: Science and Practice* 13, no. 2 (May 2006): 179–193. doi:10.1111/j.1468-2850.2006.00021.x.

Sweeney, Paul D., Karen Anderson, and Scott Bailey. "Attributional Style in Depression: A Meta-Analytic Review." *Journal of Personality and Social Psychology* 50, no. 5 (May 1986): 974–991. doi:10.1037/0022-3514.50.5.974.

Teasdale, John D., Zindel Segal, and J. Mark G. Williams. "How Does Cognitive Therapy Prevent Depressive Relapse and Why Should Attentional Control (Mindfulness) Training Help?" *Behaviour Research and Therapy* 33, no. 1 (January 1995): 25–39. doi:10.1016/0005-7967(94)E0011-7.

Tolin, David F. "Is Cognitive-Behavioral Therapy More Effective Than Other Therapies?: A Meta-Analytic Review." *Clinical Psychology Review* 30, no. 6 (August 2010): 710–720. doi:10.1016/j.cpr.2010.05.003.

Tuckman, Ari. *Integrative Treatment for Adult ADHD*. Oakland, CA: New Harbinger Publications, 2007.

Vittengl, Jeffrey R., Lee Anna Clark, Todd W. Dunn, and Robin B. Jarrett. "Reducing Relapse and Recurrence in Unipolar Depression: A Comparative Meta-Analysis of Cognitive-Behavioral Therapy's Effects." *Journal of Consulting and Clinical Psychology* 75, no. 3 (June 2007): 475–488. doi:10.1037/0022-006X.75.3.475.

Wegner, Daniel M., David J. Schneider, Samuel R. Carter, and Teri L. White. "Paradoxical Effects of Thought Suppression." *Journal of Personality and Social Psychology* 53, no. 1 (July 1987): 5–13. doi:10.1037/0022-3514.53.1.5.

Wei, Meifen, Philip A. Shaffer, Shannon K. Young, and Robyn A. Zakalik. "Adult Attachment, Shame, Depression, and Loneliness: The Mediation Role of Basic Psychological Needs Satisfaction." *Journal of Counseling Psychology* 52, no. 4 (October 2005): 591–601. doi:10.1037/0022-0167.52.4.591.

Wells, Adrian, David M. Clark, Paul Salkovskis, John Ludgate, Ann Hackmann, and Michael Gelder. "Social Phobia: The Role of In-Situation Safety Behaviors in Maintaining Anxiety and Negative Beliefs." *Behavior Therapy* 26, no. 1 (Winter 1996): 153–161. doi:10.1016/S0005-7894(05)80088-7.

Westra, Henny A., David J. A. Dozois, and Madalyn Marcus. "Expectancy, Homework Compliance, and Initial Change in Cognitive-Behavioral Therapy for Anxiety." *Journal of Consulting and Clinical Psychology* 75, no. 3 (June 2007): 363-373. doi:10.1037/0022-006X.75.3.363.

Williams, Chris, and Rebeca Martinez. "Increasing Access to CBT: Stepped Care and CBT Self-Help Models in Practice." *Behavioural and Cognitive Psychotherapy* 36, no. 6 (November 2008): 675-683. doi:10.1017/S1352465808004864.

Wolpe, Joseph. "Psychotherapy by Reciprocal Inhibition." *Conditional Reflex: A Pavlovian Journal of Research and Therapy* 3, no. 4 (October 1968): 234-240. doi:10.1007/BF03000093.

World Health Organization. "Media Centre: Depression Fact Sheet." Accessed June 23, 2016. http://www.who.int/mediacentre/factsheets/fs369/en/.

Notes

Index

Acknowledgments

I am thankful to the many individuals who have influenced the writing of this book. My mom and dad have offered words of encouragement at crucial moments throughout my life. My four brothers, Yonder, Malachi, Timothy, and Charlie, are a constant source of support, in the best and worst of times.

Two professors at The George Washington University strongly influenced my clinical training: Dr. Ray Pasi inspired me as a clinician and continues to inspire me with his warmth of spirit and sense of humor. I also received thoughtful and consistent mentoring from the late Dr. Chris Erickson, who steered me toward CBT.

As a student new to CBT at the University of Pennsylvania, I could not have had better clinical supervisors: Dr. Melissa Hunt, my assessment supervisor, taught me to trust my instincts. Dr. Alan Goldstein showed me how warmly human good behavior therapy could be. Dr. Rob DeRubeis, my cognitive therapy supervisor for three years, has a gift for supporting each trainee's unique style as a CBT therapist. I was fortunate that Dr. Dianne Chambless, who spearheaded the development of a list of treatments supported by research, was director of clinical training at Penn during my time there. Dr. Martha Farah was the world's best doctoral advisor, and fully supported my career decisions even when they led me away from academia. Dr. Edna Foa, a pioneer in anxiety treatment, provided invaluable training and collaboration while I was on the full-time faculty at Penn. I had an excellent postdoctoral supervisor in Dr. Elyssa Kushner, who introduced me to mindfulness-based therapy.

Thanks to Janet Singer for a rewarding collaboration that continues to bear fruit. I appreciate Corey Field's sound and generous counsel.

My editor, Nana K. Twumasi, was wonderful to work with and integral to the overall vision of this project.

Over the past 15 years, I've had the distinct privilege of treating hundreds of individuals committed to making difficult changes. Thank you for the opportunity to work together—I have learned immensely from you.

Finally, to my wife and friend Marcia Leithauser: I am grateful beyond words for your continual support, your insightful suggestions when I was feeling stuck, and for reminding me, from the beginning, to write from the heart.

About the Author

Licensed psychologist Seth J. Gillihan, PhD, is a Clinical Assistant Professor of Psychology in the Psychiatry Department at the University of Pennsylvania. He completed his doctorate at the University of Pennsylvania, where he trained in cognitive-behavioral therapy (CBT) and the cognitive neuroscience of mood and emotion. Dr. Gillihan has written and lectured nationally and internationally on CBT and how the brain is involved in regulating our moods. He coauthored *Overcoming OCD: A Journey to Recovery* with Janet Singer, which describes how CBT helped her son recover from severe OCD. Dr. Gillihan has a clinical practice in Haverford, Pennsylvania, where he specializes in CBT and mindfulness-based interventions for anxiety, depression, and related conditions. He lives in Ardmore, Pennsylvania, with his wife and three children. Learn more about Dr. Gillihan and find more resources at his website: http://sethgillihan.com.

About the Foreword Author

Lucy F. Faulconbridge, PhD, is a Clinical Assistant Professor of Psychology in the Center for Weight and Eating Disorders at the University of Pennsylvania's Perelman School of Medicine. She maintains a private practice in Wayne, Pennsylvania, specializing in the treatment of eating disorders, depression, and anxiety. She received her B.A. from the University of St Andrews in Scotland in 2000 and her M.A. in psychology from the University of Pennsylvania in 2002.